Stairway To Serenity

THE ELEVENTH STEP

First published October, 1988.

ISBN: 0-89486-553-6

Library of Congress Catalog Card Number: 88-82664

Printed in the United States of America.

Editor's Note:
Hazelden Educational Materials offers a variety of information on chemical dependency and related areas. Our publications do not necessarily represent Hazelden or its programs, nor do they officially speak for any Twelve Step organization.

The following publisher has generously given permission to use extended quotations from a copyrighted work: From *A Course In Miracles*. (Portions) Reprinted by Permission from *A Course In Miracles*. © Copyright 1975, Foundation for Inner Peace, Inc.

CONTENTS

Introduction 1
Brave New World 5
How It Works 11
Act As If 17
Call to Action 23
Teachers of Each Other 27
Just Be Yourself 33
Doing What Comes Naturally 37
Turn It Over 43
Appreciation 51
Dialogue with Myself 55
Ask 57
One Spirit 61
Defenselessness 67
Forgiveness 71
Now 75
Give 79
Everything's Okay 83
Summary 87
Index 91

INTRODUCTION

God grant me the serenity
To accept the things I cannot change,
The courage to change the things I can,
And the wisdom to know the difference.

The Serenity Prayer

The Serenity Prayer usually is attributed to Reinhold Niebuhr, a Twentieth-Century theologian, who in turn credited it to an Eighteenth-Century theologian, Friedrich Detinger. This prayer and variations of it have been traced as far back as 500 A.D. to the Roman philosopher Anicius Boethius. Whatever its origins, the prayer may never have graced as many tongues as it has in this century, when it was adopted by Alcoholics Anonymous and other self-help groups whose members are recovering from addiction.

Saying The Serenity Prayer is one of many ways recovering addicts remind themselves that they haven't gotten this far alone.

The prayer helps me to remember the Twelve Steps of A.A. that brought sobriety to this terribly sick alcoholic, and especially the Eleventh Step that introduced me to a way of living that is the best approximation of serenity I can imagine.

You won't find my name in this book. It is not important. Quite a few well-known authors and other prominent people are quoted by name. All others, if recovering addicts, are identified only by first name, and each of those names is fictitious. I assure you, though, that everyone named is real. And each of them has helped to uncover the real me.

As a recovering addict, I have written this book especially for people who have identified compulsive or addictive behaviors in their lives. What it has to say, though, applies to all who have suffered paralyzing physical, mental, or emotional setbacks.

1

"My Drug of Choice is *More*."

Some of us believe the object of our addiction is not the important thing, but that we have addictive personalities and are compulsive about a lot of things. In fact, many respected treatment centers in the United States teach addicts that once the disease has taken hold, they are vulnerable to other addictions.

If we look back, some of us can see that from an early age we have been driven by basic urges, such as hunger and the need for security.

A recovering addict named Frank put it this way:

"Today I don't see myself as an alcohol addict or as a drug addict, a sex addict, a love addict, a food addict, or whatever. Although I am all these things, I like to look at myself simply as an addict. My drug of choice is *more*."

For this discussion, the specific addiction isn't important. What is important is the bottom, for there is something stubborn about most human beings. No matter how unhappy we may be or how low we have fallen, we aren't often willing to stop and look at ourselves until we feel overwhelming pain or utter despair. Then and only then do we see the need for change. This is where recovery begins.

The Eleventh Step of A.A. — Spiritual Growth

We recovering addicts no longer need to be controlled by addiction. When we have been free of it for some time, we know that our continued freedom is dependent on spiritual growth. Spiritual growth is what this book is about. It has to do with what many consider to be the most profound experience we humans can have — communication with a Higher Power. This idea is rooted in the Eleventh Step of Alcoholics Anonymous: "Sought through prayer and meditation to improve our conscious contact with God *as we understood Him*, praying only for knowledge of His will for us and the power to carry that out."[1]

---

[1] *Alcoholics Anonymous* (New York: Alcoholics Anonymous World Services, Inc., 1976), 59.

Combined with the other eleven Steps in A.A.'s Twelve Steps to recovery, this Step has helped millions of alcoholics stay sober. It is no longer exclusive to A.A. People with other addictions have formed self-help groups for recovery and use the Twelve Steps with minor variations.

Actually, to label these "self"-help programs is a little misleading, for in the Eleventh Step we acknowledge that we look for help *beyond* ourselves — outside our normal, worldly experience. We look to something we call spirit. For those who have difficulty with the concept of a deity, this may be the human spirit, the spirit of love, or the spirit of brotherhood.

If we consider this spirit a Power greater than ourselves, a Higher Power that brings us inspiration, enlightenment and comfort, it doesn't matter what it's called. It works. The power of "the group," and the love from which that power flows, have given countless addicts sobriety and turned their lives around.

Most of us in Twelve Step programs who have stayed out of trouble for a while eventually moved on from the most elementary spiritual concept of love for one another, to the recognition of a spirit beyond human understanding. We were grateful for what we had received, but we suspected that there was more, and we wanted it.

For many who delved into the Eleventh Step with the idea of finding something more, the results have been startling. It wasn't just insurance against falling off the wagon; it was Sobriety Plus and then some. More about that later.

BRAVE NEW WORLD

Just how or when the change took place I cannot tell.
But as insensibly and gradually as the force of life
had been annulled within me, and I had reached my
moral death-bed, just as gradually and imperceptibly
did the energy of life come back. And what was
strange was that this energy that came back was
nothing new.

— *Leo Tolstoy*

There's a better world than the one seen through our addictions; if there weren't, someone would have had to invent it. The addictive world plays too many tricks on us. It has too much of now-you-see-it-now-you-don'ts.

This better world is kind of tricky too. It's not easy for people like me to find. But the search is worth the effort. Some of the finest people I know — the weak-willed, the bullheaded, the know-it-alls, the misfits, the disinherited, the fugitives, and the undesirables — have succeeded. They're the ones who showed me the way there.

This strange, new world is hard for me to get a fix on because it seems to be on another plane, in a different dimension, hidden by clouds of my own making. But with a little help from my friends, I'm beginning to get my bearings.

These friends of mine were the least likely people to be giving up on their old, mad world, and looking for a new one, for they had so much of themselves invested in the old. But they had to. They had run out of options.

These are sensitive people — sensitive because they had gone to such extreme lengths to indulge their senses. They had dipped the fabric of their lives into a pool of pleasure and wrung it dry.

5

And what did they have to show for it? Nothing but pain, exhaustion, and disappointment. Things weren't bringing them any happiness. Sensations weren't fulfilling their dreams.

They were beginning to think it didn't matter what they owned or how much money they had or who they took to bed or where they went for fun or how many people they could impress. They always seemed to come up empty.

Where was the pleasure? Bodies had been stroked and poked and filled to overflowing; magic elixirs swallowed, snorted, and shot into veins. The pleasure? Gone. Not a trace remained.

An actress named Myrna put it this way:

"When the booze got me down, I'd quit drinking for another two-and-a-half years and say, 'Okay, I'll stay stoned.' And then I'd go and stock up on Valium. You know what they say, 'Valium is as good as a dry martini.' It was a way for me not to have to be honest, not to have to feel, not to have to be grown up."

That was happening to a lot of these people. So it was time for them to get out. This wasn't the way it was supposed to be.

Somewhere, they said, there had to be a better world, a saner world. There had to be a higher *something*. And then, in desperation, and often quite by accident, they found it — where they had never dreamed of looking for it.

Little Bit Moore Meets Themanwho

A speaker at a meeting of doctors, nurses, and counselors on the topic of addiction told about a character named Little Bit Moore. The speaker said everybody in his hometown knew the story, and he swore it was true.

Little Bit Moore had tried it all, every drug known: purple mushrooms and banana peels, Listerine on ice, beer through a straw, LSD, PCP and all the rest of the alphabet soup, but none of it was quite enough. What he needed was just a little bit more. When he heard about a holy man in the Himalayas who was said to possess the secret of the ultimate high, he sailed across the ocean, slogged through jungle swamps, and climbed mountain trails. At last, high upon a ledge he found Themanwho, a guru of great renown, who proceeded to tell him that there was no secret. "The ultimate high," he said, "is to be found within." Sure that Themanwho was putting him on, Little Bit Moore insisted he divulge the real secret, upon which Themanwho demanded all of Little Bit's worldly goods. He then told him about the bark of the Colorado aspen tree. "Those who partake of the dust of the dried bark of the aspen," said Themanwho, "will achieve the ultimate high."

So, with great elation, Little Bit Moore climbed down and began his journey back to America to find the aspen tree, leaving Themanwho on his mountain, pondering the ways of human nature. He sat there a moment, then looked up and asked, "Why, oh Lord, is it so much easier to sell them some crap than to give them the truth?"

The friends I get my advice from are a little closer to home than Themanwho, but they're not much different, I'm afraid, than Little Bit Moore.

These advisers, like Little Bit and me, are all addicts. But unlike Little Bit, they have begun to find the secret of the ultimate high is, just as Themanwho said, *within themselves*.

On-Time Kathleen

Her nickname doesn't come from being punctual, but that's another story. On-Time Kathleen came into A.A. despondent and she didn't get over it in a hurry. But let her tell it:

"The first few years in this program, I was very unhappy, very confused, very angry, and very depressed. You know, a thousand things. I was also suicidal. Here I was sober, and I really wanted to die. One of the thoughts that came to me (and I clung to it ever after, getting through that hard time) was, *I can't check out right now because I don't know what's around the next corner. I've got to wait and see.* And what I found around the next corner was something of beauty, a new way of being alive.

"So no matter what happens in my life I know there's always going to be something different and exciting, maybe more wonderful than anything that's happened so far."

In saying that, On-Time Kathleen speaks for a lot of addicts.

We addicts come in all shapes and sizes, and all guises. In more than a dozen years of being sober, I've heard a lot of stories and been witness to more than a few miracles. I've seen amazing personality transformations, maybe even the creation of a saint or two. There's not one who would claim sainthood, but most would gladly say, "I owe it all to being an addict." They mean that addiction was their introduction to the spiritual world, to a peace of mind unlike anything they had ever found in the material world.

The two worlds are not really separate, of course, except in our perception of them. Both are aspects of human existence. It's just that our spiritual awareness — along with any hope for peace of mind tends to be blotted out by our addictions.

I've been around addicts for most of my adult life. As an alcoholic, I guzzled booze with them in many a bar, and shook and trembled and hallucinated with them in a few hospitals and detox clinics. Now, as a volunteer worker at a treatment center, I have a different perspective. But addicts remain the same. Some readily accept help and some stubbornly rebuff it. The difference is often in the degree of desperation they feel.

Many will never make it out of the clutches of their disease. They may not even reach the fork in the road that offers them a choice of destination and won't get a chance to try a Twelve Step program. But those who do are beginning to change the world around them.

Because of the transformation I've seen in some of them, once their feet were set on the spiritual path by the Twelve Steps, I have great hope for this new generation of addicts. With professional assistance and the variety of Twelve Step programs available, there are opportunities addicts not so long ago wouldn't have dreamed of. And yet the Twelve Step principles have been around a long time and are available to all whose desperation has brought them to seek a spiritual way of life.

This is why the program works: not by being an esoteric movement, cult, or religion, but by offering the possibility for good, solid, everyday spiritual experience. It turns no one away and can transform anyone willing to give it an honest try.

Addicts or not, when we come in desperation, defeat, or surrender with a desire to stay clean and sober, to overcome our fears or whatever it is that has us whipped, we are welcomed.

HOW IT WORKS

Having seen through Watergate how vulnerable man
can be, I no longer believe I am master of my
destiny. I need God; I need friends with whom I can
honestly share my failures and feelings of inadequacy.

— *Charles W. Colson*
Born Again

Abner was a physician at the county health department. His name had been in the paper several times in connection with treatment of the AIDS virus. He came in one night hanging his head and nodding as people spoke to him. This wasn't like Abner. He usually had a smile for everyone. It was a Step meeting and the Step for this night was the Eleventh: "Sought through prayer and meditation to improve our conscious contact with God *as we understood Him,* praying only for knowledge of His will for us and the power to carry that out."

It was an upbeat meeting. Several of us had shared evidence that our Higher Power had taken a hand in our lives. By the time the discussion came around to Abner, we were set for more of the same. We didn't get it.

"I'm Abner," he said, "an addict and alcoholic. I've been thinking about some of the things we say in these meetings. Like,'Thy will be done, not mine.' And 'Everything that happens has a meaning.' These topics have been really on my mind the last few weeks. The last couple of weekends, I've spent walking the beach, trying to sort it out.

"Many of you know I deal with people with the AIDS virus. This year, I've been reporting an average of three people a month. Last year it was two a month; the year before it was one a month. Tomorrow I've got to face a twenty-three-year-old kid and tell him that his blood work is half as good as it was six months ago. He's starting the inevitable decline."

By this time Abner was looking down, just kind of mumbling. He appeared to be in great pain. "Uh, I keep telling myself there's a meaning behind all this." After a pause, he said, "I don't know what it is. I just don't know."

Abner was seated next to Anabel, a beautiful young woman with long, pale blonde hair, who worked for an organization that cares for dying people. "I'd like to share something with you," Anabel said.

"I'm a hospice nurse, and I think you were given your talent for a reason," she said to Abner. "I'm grateful there are people like you who are willing to feel their pain. I wouldn't want someone in that position who wouldn't feel it. That would be horrible to be gravely ill and have someone you depend on for information and medical care be shallow and cold."

I called Abner the next day. He was feeling better. He was on top of things again. "I'm glad I went to that meeting," he said. "It meant a lot that someone cared."

That's how it works. The people we need appear when we need them and they seem to say what we need to hear. Is it coincidental? Only if you want it to be.

The Twelve Step programs for addicts are self-help programs. They show us how to get help for ourselves by going to the One who can do all things and that One often comes to us through our friends.

Bob, my sponsor, said:

"I remember the night when I said for the first time, 'I'm an alcoholic.' I felt something change in me. Many months later, when I took the Fifth Step, I was upset, and I was fighting it as I sat in a parked car in Yonkers, New York, with my sponsor. But I shared some things I had never shared with anybody before, and that was a big, big turning point for me, because since then there hasn't been anything that I haven't been able to share, with somebody. For some of us, it's the beginning of a relationship with some kind of Higher Power."

When it comes to trying spiritual things, a lot of us hold back because we're not sure of doing it right and the results are hard to tally. For one thing, we're trying to get help from a source we can't see. We're also programmed from childhood to depend on our own wits: we got ourselves into this pickle and we can get ourselves out. At least that's what we thought until we finally had to admit we were licked.

"I had a great deal of difficulty believing in a Power Greater than Howard," said Howard, a Massachusetts state government bureaucrat. "But eventually I became like that scientist they talk about: he's afraid to make experiments for fear he'll find the answers. I think that's the way I was with God. I was afraid to find there was something other than Howard that had something to do with Howard's life."

Our addictions made us afraid of a lot of things. We expected the worst and usually got it. Now that we're recovering, we know that doesn't have to be. We've seen miracles. We've seen derelicts, degenerates, and strung-out zombies transformed into bright, grateful, loving human beings. Not many of us who have been around meeting rooms for a while can say we're the same people we were when we first came.

For some of us, that's enough. Compared to our past, that's more than enough. But we can't stand still even though, for some of us, it may be slow going.

"Generally, I find myself going through the day with the right kind of attitude," says an alcoholic named Frank. "And then one small incident might screw up the whole day. I have to watch my attitude constantly. I have to remember who I am, what I am, where I am, and why I'm where I am. It's because I can sink into trouble and enjoy it; I think normal people don't get that happy about being in deep trouble. And everybody says,'Oh, isn't that terrible,' yet *I* feel good about it. I'm like those people in Iran that I saw on TV, marching down the street and whipping themselves; it's just I never had a parade!"

"No one among us has been able to maintain anything like perfect adherence to these principles [the Twelve Steps]," says the "Big Book," *Alcoholics Anonymous*. "We are not saints. The point is, that we are willing to grow along spiritual lines. The principles we have set down are guides to progress. We claim spiritual progress rather than spiritual perfection."

So it's spiritual progress we're after. Continual adherence to the Twelve Steps will ensure that progress, especially if we pay close attention to the Second, Third, Eleventh, and Twelfth Steps. In the Second Step we, maybe for the first time, acknowledge our insanity and the possibility that there's a Power greater than us that can restore us. We'll talk more about that in the next section.

In the Third Step, we continually renew our decision to turn our life over to the care of God, as we understand Him. That's a tricky thing to do, but there are ways to do it that have worked for many of us, and we'll be talking about some of them.

In the Eleventh Step, we seek to improve our conscious contact with that Power, which is what this book is really about.

In the Twelfth Step, we practice the principles we've learned and try to help others. Of the four Steps, this is the one that probably gets the most results, because it's a "people" Step. We put what we've learned into action and teach others by how we live. In this way, as long as we live, our spiritual progress will continue.

We come again to a recurring theme in our journey: the spiritual life is not some nebulous state that is attainable only by the cloistered. It is not a formal religious process or an esoteric calling. It is available to us all. We can have it for breakfast and take it to work with us. We can use it throughout the day to make us brighter and more successful. We can use it to make our relationships — any contact with another person — work. Throughout the day, it is the difference between harmony and discord.

It's for everybody, addict and nonaddict. Addicts are just a little more fortunate. We're like the mule after the farmer has bounced a two-by-four off her head: now that he has our attention, we're more inclined to listen.

Jenny is paying attention now. A young, recovering drug addict, she told this story of faith-in-the-making:

"Last week, I was in a bad way and I really needed to talk to this person I'd met who'd been able to give me some hope for the first time in a long time. All I knew was that she was in the program. I didn't know where she went to meetings or anything. So I thought I'd go down to the club, and all the way down I prayed that somebody would be at a meeting. I didn't even know if there was a meeting there that day, but I thought maybe somebody there would know how to contact this person. And then, when I first got there, my heart fell. There were two lousy cars. One belonged to the person who makes the coffee. And then as I got closer I recognized the other one. It belonged to the person I was looking for. That's how it works."

I'll be talking about other everyday miracles in the course of this book and about specific actions that help us in our spiritual progress. I'll be talking about things that have worked for others, not theories. I'll try to avoid getting too philosophical or speculative and just stick pretty much to what works.

ACT AS IF

When it becomes clear that you cannot find out by reasoning whether the cat is in the linen-cupboard, it is Reason herself who whispers, "Go and look. This is not my job: it is a matter for the senses."

— C. S. Lewis

The Second Step wasn't easy for some of us, even those who had started out with some exposure to religion.

"Came to believe that a Power greater than ourselves could restore us to sanity." Power with a capital "P." That can be scary for some, infuriating for others.

What about us nonbelievers? We have to believe in some nebulous "Power" and at the same time admit we're nuts? A tall order.

When Andy from New York recited his revulsion at the idea of "A God who had permitted a gang of immoral followers to parade for centuries under the 'Three-M' banner — myths, magic, and miracles, — all a bunch of ridiculous nonsense," his sponsor just smiled and nodded. He had heard it before. And he said Andy didn't have to believe any of that stuff.

To stay sober and clean, we don't have to believe anyone's theology. All we have to do is follow the suggestions found in our Twelve Step programs.

One of the nice things about action is that it doesn't require faith. If we take the Twelve Steps one at a time, it doesn't matter what we believe when we start out. When we use the Steps, applying them to our lives, something invariably happens, something changes. We need not know the source of the change and we don't have to worship it. We don't even have to believe that anything will happen.

"It's always been hard for me to talk about God," a visitor named Ron said at a meeting one night. "I think one of the reasons for that is that not only am I an alcoholic, but I'm a child of an alcoholic. We don't talk about that much in these rooms.

"But that's one of the reasons I have trouble with a Higher Power," Ron said, "because when I was a little kid 'Higher Powers' weren't very reliable. Oh, it's a great idea, God is a great idea. It just never seemed to work in my life.

"But I have to admit, the more time I spend in this program, the more opportunities I have to listen to other people talk about their successful experiences with taking risks and applying faith and stuff like that, the more inclined I am to try it myself."

If doubters hang around meeting rooms long enough, they'll see people undergoing change. They'll see timidity changing to confidence, despondency changing to hope, fear changing to love.

Acting Crazy

In some parts of California they talk about out-of-control drunks off on a spree as being "crazy in the streets." After Andy had returned from an unscheduled trip back to the streets, his sponsor said, "Let's not argue about a Higher Power we can't see. You can see a bottle of hooch. Do you admit that this stuff is more powerful than you are?"

Andy mumbled and nodded. "How about this group? Is it more powerful than the booze?"

Andy looked around. He'd been in the group a few months before he went back to the streets. He had made friends with a number of people who had told of drinking themselves into the DTs, comas, convulsions, and worse. Some of them were healthy, happy-go-lucky, joyful, and had been alcohol-free for several years. A couple were well into their third decade of sobriety.

"I guess I have to," Andy said. "Whatever's been happening here has got booze beat. At least for them."

"Okay," said his sponsor, "let A.A. be your Higher Power, let this group be your Higher Power."

As for being nuts, it's not terribly important that we dwell on our former craziness, but it ought to be self-evident.

"When I first came into this program, I did not think I was insane," says Suzie, a free-lance news photographer. "I had other names for the things I did, you see. Sneaking into South American countries with no passport, that was adventure, not insanity. Sleeping with a gun under my pillow was security, not insanity. I had all these other names for these crazy things that I did."

A young mother, Cherry, said that she came in "as an agnostic, and when I saw the words 'could restore us to sanity' that became my rallying point. I did not think I was an alcoholic, I just thought I was crazy. I was having a lot of blackouts; there were things like not recognizing my two-year-old daughter. Only crazy people could do some of the things I did. And then the route of shrinks, psychiatrists, psychologists, marriage counseling, and none of it gave me any relief.

"But then something hit me after I had been sober four or five years," Cherry continued. "Where it says 'God could and would if He were sought,' and that for everybody in A.A. there's a different opinion of God. That freed me so I could begin to seek a lot more, and I began to do some of it outside of A.A., and it added a dimension to my program and that has really been a blessing. I know I never would have found Him if it hadn't been for my alcoholism. And for that I'm really grateful. Only He could have turned something so rotten into such a blessing."

Acting Our Way into a New Way Of Thinking

The program's oldtimers, too, have no doubt that they acted crazy. And while most of them today do enjoy a personal faith in a Higher Power beyond the group, they'll tell us it's not necessary. The oldtimers tell us we don't have to have a faith. If we're having trouble, they suggest we fake it and go through the motions.

Fake it? Why, sure.

Act as if, they say.

Act as if you're sane.

Act as if there is Divine Order in the universe.

Act as if there is Someone watching over you.

Act as if your smile will be returned.

Wilbur, a cocaine addict in Fort Lauderdale, said he had a lot of trouble with the Twelve Step program at first. He tried his intellect on it, but as many have discovered, there's no way to intellectualize inner peace.

"Changing beliefs came as a by-product," Wilbur said. "I found I could not think my way into a new way of acting, but that I could act my way into a new way of thinking."

The same thing happened to Rob, an alcoholic from Georgia. He said he grew up with religion, "but I didn't have any spirituality. So when I first came into this program, what I wanted to do was understand it, and when I could understand it, then I thought I would be able to do it.

"When I got to the place where I would try what you people told me to do — when I *acted as if it would work,* on the basis of faith — was when I had the key in the door and suddenly I began to recover."

Rob lives near Cape Canaveral now. "Every day as I go to work," he says, "I have the privilege of riding along several miles of the Indian River. A lot of times the sun is just coming up and the water has a nice rosy glow to it. Pelicans are sitting around the docks. And I get a beautiful feeling from that inside. The ability to have that feeling to me is spiritual; so is the feeling that God is doing something for me that I couldn't do for myself, because I was unable to feel those things until I had a spiritual program for myself.

"Before," Rob says, "I always approached the program on an intellectual basis, and I would only accept those parts of the program that looked like they made sense intellectually. And then after I had started to accept it on the basis of faith I realized that there is no purely intellectual basis for the program. It's a group of *spiritual actions,* and if I'm willing to take those spiritual actions then there will be spiritual results."

Spiritual actions equal spiritual results. As simple as that.

Faith Comes From the Heart

A Chinese proverb says of God: "By love He may be gotten and held, but by thought never."

Our agnostic friend Andy came to similar conclusions. After a couple of years, he began reciting "The Lord's Prayer" along with other members at the close of meetings. And, after some particularly trying times, he found himself on his knees each night at home.

"What a change!" he said. "I had finally come to see that my pride in my intellect blocked my faith in a Higher Power. All my years of education, the prodigious amounts of reading I had done, all had created a conviction that any idea, any theory that cannot be proved by the scientific method had to be false, and that I owed it to my intellectual integrity to reject it. Intellectual honesty was everything.

"In my insufferable pride I had overlooked the simple fact that most of a human being's behavior patterns are established not by intelligence but by emotion — not in our heads but in our guts. I remember my friend Earl saying over and over, meeting after meeting, 'If it's wrong, I know it — I feel it in my gut.' Now I know it's all right to listen to my feelings. I can believe in a divinity without having to believe in all the rituals and trappings of organized religion."

When Bill W. wrote the first draft of the Twelve Steps of A.A., he put a great emphasis on God. Five of the Steps referred to God and another Step had us "humbly on our knees." Bill W. was talked into modifying the concept of a Higher Power by a handful of early members, so that the Steps now speak of "God as we understood Him."

Bill W. was grateful for this advice. He called it "the great contribution of our atheists and agnostics. They had widened our gateway so that all who suffer might pass through, regardless of their belief or *lack of belief.*"

21

But that didn't relieve the nonbelievers of their duty to themselves to put what they had learned into action. And, for believer and nonbeliever alike, to "act as if."

"To believe in God is to desire his existence," wrote the Spanish philosopher Miguel de Unamuno, "and what is more, to act as though He existed."

"It is not the image we create of God which proves God," echoed Pierre Lecomte du Noüy, the French scientist and philosopher. "It is the effort we make to create this image."

CALL TO ACTION

Love is the highest and holiest action, because it always contains that which is not love within itself, it always and ever moves to include the unloving.

— *Thaddeus Golas*
Lazy Man's Guide to Enlightenment

Action is how we know what works. We've heard a lot of good things from our fellow addicts. They offer us a lot of good advice. We didn't necessarily think that at first. In fact, as shaken and demoralized as we were when we first came to these groups, we may have even believed there was a thing or two they could learn from us, especially as we put more distance between ourselves and our addictions.

If we were lucky, though, we got over that cockiness. We learned to be still and listen. We learned how to learn. Being able to gain some trust, to put some confidence in what another person was saying, was a gift.

When other people shared their experience, strength, and hope with us, we knew what they were talking about. We were learning all over again how to be honest. How to make amends. How to forgive. And maybe, just maybe, how to love. Just thinking about these lofty ideals made us feel good. What a change over what we used to think about and talk about.

But there comes a time when thinking isn't good enough and we've talked ourselves out. There comes a time for action. For some of us, action meant Twelfth Step work. We responded to calls for help from addicts still out in the cold. We paired up with a senior member of the group and made house calls. We made comparisons:

The poor sucker sitting there on the side of the bed, shaking to pieces — that was me! Boy, am I glad I'm not there now. My heart goes out to him. What can I do for you, pal? I'll stay here with you and help you stay off the stuff. Then we'll go to a meeting tonight. It's a start.

It's also a glimpse of what love is like.

This kind of work is absolutely necessary. This is the way we repay the love we have received. But Twelfth Step calls are not often a part of our daily routine.

The Program at Work in Our Daily Lives

Principles are fine but what do they have to do with our jobs and our home life? Theory is useless until we put it into practice. We have to see if it works.

But then we often find that we get busy on the job. There doesn't seem to be time to think about principles when we have a run-in with a fellow worker and anger flares or the boss criticizes our work and we start worrying about how we'll get another job. And there's home, where the kids are full of mischief and won't do what they're told and our mates don't understand what we're going through.

We wonder where our self-confidence went. What happened to that serenity that seemed so real in the meeting the other night?

If we can't find it in our daily lives what good is it?

At this point, if we're smart, we do what we've been told. We talk to our sponsor, or our closest friend, and ask what we're doing wrong. We ask for help, just as we did when we first admitted we were powerless over our addiction.

In A.A., the usual advice is, "Don't drink and keep coming to meetings." Sometimes it's, "Don't ask me. You need help from a Power greater than I am."

You may not always hear an answer, particularly if you're praying for "things" just for yourself like better health or more money.

How about my character traits, then? Can they be changed merely by asking? I doubt it, and especially not if I'm sitting on my backside and expecting God to do my bidding. Unfortunately this is not an unfamiliar posture for me, lounging around, calling the shots.

Why should He help if all I'm interested in is whining about my character defects? I'm a good backseat driver. "Take a left at the next block, God." Maybe I ought to do more than give directions. Maybe I ought to *ask* directions — and then carry them out.

And how do I go about doing that?

When I ask for help with a personal problem, and no one else is involved, hearing the answer, if there is one, is difficult. When I ask for help with a relationship, though, something happens.

Relationships, even a brief encounter with a stranger, seem always to be blessed if I ask my Higher Power to handle them. Asking for help enables me to go into the encounter with an attitude of helpfulness — an attitude of trying to get along.

It's in the interaction, the participation in something outside myself that makes the answer real.

Help comes with the action of asking, particularly if it is for a specific relationship or a specific person. Action triggers it.

And I can take that action anytime I want. I don't have to wait until bedtime or my morning meditations to ask.

"I find," says Sarah, an audiologist, "that whether I set my quiet time aside in the morning, or at night when I'm going to bed, I get results either way. For me, it's not a matter of time of the day; I think it's the fact that I've *taken the action* to go do it."

I try to listen to the voice of my inner guide. It's hard to distinguish it from the voice of my ego, the voice of my selfishness, the voice of my fear. I have only one sure way of identifying it: put the advice into action. If it works, I know I was listening to the right voice. If it doesn't I have to choose again.

I learn something about love when I try to respond with love to another person's anger or irrationality. I can think about a calm, caring response as the mature thing to do. But put me in a room with a hostile person and my impulse is to bristle. I can think about being kind, considerate, and understanding, but it doesn't mean a thing if I don't actually do it. When I can say a quick prayer, then try to make my actions calm and caring, I get help.

Putting these thoughts on paper is one way of teaching myself what I need to know about my Higher Power. But I wouldn't have found that out if I hadn't started doing it. I am taught through action.

TEACHERS OF EACH OTHER

There is guidance for each of us, and by lowly listening, we shall hear the right word.

— *Ralph Waldo Emerson*

People who write books on how to improve a golf swing, or how to develop a backhand in tennis may be natural athletes. People who teach courses on how to invest in the stock market or how to make money in real estate may also be naturally endowed. Such talents, unfortunately, are not always transferable, no matter how skillful the teacher.

The same may go for spiritual advisers. Someone we know may have a deep, abiding faith, and may be a walking demonstration of the presence of God. But while we can learn from a person like this, we have to come by our spirituality in our own way. There are no tricks. Although some people may seem further along or naturally inclined toward spirituality, that is of no concern to us. Our ultimate concern is for our own spiritual life.

"I think it's nice for people who have a religion," says Karen, a Catholic widow who shared nearly two dozen years of sobriety with her husband in A.A. He was her companion and her great comfort all those years. But of even more comfort was what she found in the program. It helped her survive his death.

"I think the power you find in this program maybe enhances religion," Karen added. "But the primary power for me is here."

This veiled skepticism toward religion is possibly the same thing some addicts feel toward counselors who haven't tasted their particular brand of poison. C.C. Nuckolls, a drug treatment consultant, asked this question of a group of therapists: "What happens when a cocaine addict walks into your office and says, 'Last night I went out and free-based my brains out'? And you look at him, not quite understanding what he's saying, and you say, 'Free-base that's the stuff you smoke, isn't it?' I mean you've lost your credibility!"

Most people didn't understand alcoholics back in the early thirties either. The great power of Alcoholics Anonymous, of course, blossomed from the discovery that only fellow sufferers can really know what it's like. We have felt each other's pain and confusion. We have seen one another's hallucinations.

When my high-bottom friend Albert called A.A. and an alcoholic named Charlie went to see him, Albert says that Charlie's story wasn't the same as his. "His alcoholism, the way he got to his last drink, was different from mine," Albert says. "But what I picked up as he talked to me was that he felt like I did. And I felt like he did."

We speak each other's anguish. We know what hopelessness means.

So when one of us gets sober and stays that way, we are impressed. We want to know how he or she did it. And when we find that the person got help from a Higher Power, we're willing to give it some thought.

But there's still a lot of skepticism. "Anytime I've had any involvement in religion, I've been disappointed in the people," said Mike, a young alcoholic who came into the program mad at the world. "Once I was able to make the distinction between religion and spirituality and to let go, then I began to feel the power."

When we're able to sit up and take spiritual nourishment, to be spoon-fed by our fellow addicts, we can listen to what they have to say, and take seriously what those who went before us think about the spiritual life.

Reading as a Tool for Spiritual Growth

In addition to a monthly magazine, *The Grapevine*, in which A.A.'s frequently write of their spiritual experiences, a small body of literature has sprung up around the program. It began with the works of cofounder Bill W. and was elaborated on by some of A.A.'s historians and other interpreters both inside and outside the program.

Most of us recovering addicts go to our own favorite program veterans for spiritual advice — our sponsors, certain people in our Twelve Step groups, and those who have written about their spiritual adventures. Then, after awhile, having heard that veteran members also get help from outside readings, a lot of us begin exploring.

Many of us belong to churches and we gravitate toward their teachings. We may find favorite writers on spirituality who inspire us and whose teachings are supportive of our Twelve Step philosophy. Emmet Fox, Emerson Fosdick, Ernest Holmes, Norman Vincent Peale, and, more recently, an anonymous collection of writings called *A Course in Miracles* (which I'll say more about later) are some that I've turned to. We tend to welcome the writings of anyone who discusses spiritual principles that we can use to improve our conscious contact with God as we understand Him.

"I was going to a meeting in Worcester," said a Massachusetts farmer named Al. "I was sober probably four years; it was a rainy night and I was going to my regular Step meeting. Something just said to me: 'Don't go to the Step meeting; go visit your uncle John.' I went up to see my uncle, and another miracle in my life of sobriety occurred.

"There were three boxes on the sofa. Uncle John walked over to the middle box, came up with a book, turned around, put it in my hand and said, 'Your aunt would have liked you to have this book. I think you're going to enjoy it.' 'What is it?' I asked. 'Just take it,' he said.

"And we talked awhile and I went home. I believe we get what we should get in this program. That particular book was put in my hands, it's been over five years ago, and I have used that book in my Eleventh Step meditations ever since. I never get tired of it, I never get bored with it. I always find something new even using it on a daily basis.

"I've gotten to the point where when I'm meditating in the morning I read words that are particularly moving to me that day. They move some part of me. They touch me. And I take the time to write that down. They just overpower me when I read them. So I have a journal of things that overpower me, and on a regular basis I go back to the journal and read them. They help me to be the type of person that I think my Higher Power wants me to be."

There is a message somewhere for each of us, something that seems to speak directly to us: You will find yours. It will come to you, and you'll recognize it when you see it. It will seem as if it was devised for you alone. It may not be in a particular book or church, but you'll find it.

We Are All Teachers of Each Other

Some of us find that the spiritual experiences described in a book or sermon are, like those of the tennis pro, not transferable. We give in to a suspicion about clerics or other spiritual experts that, because of their training and experience, they are so far ahead of us that we could never quite catch up. Some of us feel they know things that we'll never be privy to — that they wouldn't be in this line of work if they weren't somehow born to it, or especially blessed or endowed, making their particular experience unavailable to the rest of us.

Taking spiritual lessons from someone who has spent a lifetime on his knees is like taking driving lessons from Mario Andretti. Somehow, you don't ever feel you're gripping the steering wheel quite right.

Therefore, many of us end up exploring the spiritual life on a kind of hit-or-miss basis on our own. And yet, once we've embarked, it isn't as hard as we thought to find the way. Many have gone before us, leaving notched trees along the trail to follow.

And none of us needs to take this journey alone. We have our sponsors and other friends in our Twelve Step programs. And each of us is qualified to lead the way at any given time. Our credentials are the experience, strength, and hope of pioneers who went before us. None of us will reach perfection, but we make progress as we learn to rely on each other. And as each of us succeeds in doing that, look at how many other imperfect souls are encouraged to try.

"We are all teachers of each other," says Gerald G. Jampolsky. Dr. Jampolsky is a psychiatrist formerly on the faculty of the University of California Medical Center in San Francisco, and the founder of the Center for Attitudinal Healing in Tiburon, California. Dr. Jampolsky has written a book called, fittingly, *Love Is Letting Go of Fear*.

One A.A. historian has commented:

"This finding that, somehow, sick, disturbed people could help each other in small peer groups without the benefit of professional assistance surprised us very much . . . in such groups the helper seems to get as much help as the person being helped."

That's how A.A. and all the other self-help, Twelve Step programs work. Relatively few addicts have depended on holy people for spiritual progress. Neither have many journeyed to recovery solely through a particular school of psychotherapy. Our help has come through each other, and with the help of a Higher Power each of us finds our way.

But can a spiritual "illiterate" actually chart a spiritual course? Thank God, yes. My sponsor, a deeply spiritual man who knows virtually nothing of formalized religion and who came into A.A. as an agnostic, charted my course not so much by what he told me (although he told me plenty), as by how he lives. The personal concern and helpfulness that he extends to everyone who comes into our groups is a demonstration of purest love.

Thousands of us in the program have shown it's possible for amateur celestial navigators to weave their way through the galaxies of the spiritual universe.

I don't claim to have any special qualifications for doing a book on spirituality. I am simply a recovering alcoholic who has enjoyed some spiritual growth by practicing the Twelve Steps. The authority for what is written here comes from a "Power greater than myself," as described by people far more advanced spiritually than me. The thoughts expressed here, therefore, aren't original; whatever value there is comes from the collective wisdom of these people and from some of the writings that have been important to me in my search.

We in recovery often find ourselves doing new things with un-expected results. And this is the surest way to free ourselves of our addictions: to pass on what we've learned. That's how we stay free.

We learn from each other that it's possible, if not to reach our spiritual destination in twelve easy lessons, at least to make satis-fying progress. And that it's possible, together, to get through one day after another with a measure of calm, a modicum of confidence, a feeling of serenity.

JUST BE YOURSELF

Two errors: (1) To take everything literally,
(2) To take everything spiritually.

— *Blaise Pascal*
Pensees

It was too much of a mental struggle to be called a morning meditation. I had risen early and was sitting in my darkened living room, thinking how hard it was to make any spiritual progress. And thinking how much of that might be my fault, and how much I could lay to God's bringing me along in His own good time.

And I remembered the Sixth Step meeting of the week before, in which three or four of the guys I respect told of coming to the conclusion, after communicating with their Higher Power, that it was their responsibility to clean up their own acts.

This was a theme that had run through more than one meeting, and I didn't understand it. I was baffled that for years I had heard so many solid A.A.s say they believed in a Higher Power but weren't going to rely on it to do what they considered to be their own tasks.

"Were entirely ready to have God remove all these defects of character."

That's what the Sixth Step says. It's not hard to understand. It says we were ready *to have God* remove the defects. If there was any removing to be done, God would do it. Our only action is to get ready. So where does this idea come from, that's so common among us, that it's up to us?

Just last week, there was Jersey John, a derelict from the streets of Newark, one who almost didn't make it, but who now was healthy and prosperous, a quarter of a century sober, solid as a rock, saying that progress in overcoming character defects was accomplished by "the work that we put into it ourselves."

Here's how Joe, an ex-con, put it:

"I was willing to have God remove my defects. 'Here, God,' I said, 'you take them.' I mean He just told me flat out, they're yours, they're not mine. *I* had to work on them."

There was a retired railroad engineer named Jonesy who said:

"I don't get rid of character defects by asking Him to take them away. The defects that I've gotten rid of I did by looking hard at myself, by coming into these meetings, by talking to human beings, by getting my butt in a jam, et cetera, et cetera. As far as me asking God to remove these character defects, and thinking He's going to come in and wave a magic wand and say, 'They're gone, they're gone,' I ain't buying it."

And here is Vince, a successful yacht salesman:

"I prayed to God, 'Help me not to be a liar.' And He, in my mind, seemed to throw it right back at me."

That's what I was thinking this morning, as I sat meditating in the soft glow of early morning light: *What is the role of will in spiritual progress? Why don't we take God at His word and let Him do it?*

Bill W. wrote in the *Twelve Steps and Twelve Traditions* that this effort to be "entirely ready" was A.A.'s "way of stating the best possible attitude one can take in order to make a beginning on this lifetime job. This does not mean that we expect all our character defects to be lifted out of us as the drive to drink was."[1]

But I had to ask, "Why not, Bill?" If He lifted our compulsion to drink, to snort, to shoot up, to pig out — why wouldn't He lift the compulsion to criticize, to dominate, to demean and all the rest? Why shouldn't we believe He would? And why shouldn't we ask Him to, considering how slow our progress is on our own? How slow, at least, is mine.

Those were my troubled feelings. I mused on my failures to come to grips with my shameful feelings — hatred toward one,

---

[1] *Twelve Steps and Twelve Traditions,* (New York: A.A. World Services, Inc., 1964), 66.

fear toward another. And why had not God lifted these emotions from me, though I had repeatedly asked? Wasn't I doing my part? I didn't know because I didn't know what my part was. How does one turn off hatred? How does one relinquish fear?

I thought of anger and how it seemed to be just another form of fear, and how uncontrollable both seemed to be. Then it dawned on me as the sun dawned on the world outside my window that, in some way, love had to be the answer. Fear, I had been told, was an absence of love. Or that love was the antidote of fear. And all the trying in the world to be a better person would avail me nothing until I embraced love . . . or let go of fear.

Jampolsky's book, *Love Is Letting Go of Fear,* was my introduction to *A Course in Miracles,* which had made the Eleventh Step come alive for me for the first time in a decade of sobriety.

These exceptional writings in *A Course in Miracles* have opened a pathway of communication with my Higher Power and have changed the way I see myself and the world about me. They have brought about a kind of thought reversal that I never imagined possible and are the inspiration for many of the basic ideas in this book. I am able now, at times, to see everyone in the same light as I see my A.A. friends. I know something about the brotherhood of all people. To a large extent, fear has left me.

And yet some remains. Fear and anger. Both were embodied in the feelings I had toward a woman I worked for. There were times when she was unreasonable. There were times when she made no sense, when I could not understand what she meant; she might as well have been speaking Swahili.

This was particularly frustrating because we worked for a publishing company; communication was our business. She was an extremely bright woman yet could not make herself clear at times. Or I was too thick-headed to understand what she meant. Either way, it was maddening. I sometimes feared I wouldn't be able to carry out her instructions and that my job was in jeopardy. I got furious at her convoluted thought processes, which I attributed to the peculiarities of the female mentality. Never mind that there were other women at work who made perfectly good sense. The notion fed my anger and gave me some perverse pleasure. I sometimes caught myself reveling in anger. I cultivated my resentment and could not turn it loose when I tried.

Resentment. The one thing an alcoholic cannot afford, no matter how long sober.

As long as fear is still running my life, or aspects of it, how can I experience the full inner peace, the complete serenity that I have come to believe is the reward for practicing the Eleventh Step?

I believe that love conquers fear. I've seen it happen. And anger, too, for anger is born of fear.

All I have to do, then, is love — by letting go of fear. Let down my guard. Let love flow. As simple as that. Let go. If we are not just expressions of love, but love itself ("You are only love," says *A Course in Miracles*), then the solution is simple: be myself.

Easier said than done. How to let go of fear? How to be oneself? Surely this will require divine help. And, of course, that's what the Eleventh Step is for.

DOING WHAT COMES NATURALLY

Love is energy of life.

— Robert Browning

When the founders of Alcoholics Anonymous learned to take shelter in each one's understanding of the pain the other was experiencing, and to help fellow addicts through their long nights of fear, unwittingly they had begun plugging into the greatest force in the universe.

The love of one alcoholic for another made them strong. It gave them power all out of proportion to any former effort of will. It was like discovering electricity and learning what awesome things it can do.

Love, a sentimental emotion associated with tenderness — just the opposite of toughness — was proven to be the invincible armor that could withstand the merciless onslaught of an alcoholic compulsion. Insane impulses to drink, which had been irresistible before, were suddenly thwarted.

"As I crossed the threshold of the dining room," said one of A.A.'s pioneers, describing in the book, *Alcoholics Anonymous,* the onset of his last binge, "the thought came to mind that it would be nice to have a couple of cocktails with dinner. That was all. Nothing more."

Later, coming to in a hospital "with unbearable mental and physical suffering," he reflected on that impulse. "Not only had I been off guard, I had made no fight whatever against the first drink. This time I had not thought of the consequences at all."

This after a lifetime of drunken sprees that always started with the innocent thought that a drink would be nice. What could it hurt? What a strange thought. Insanity, pure and simple.

Hospitals, psychiatrists, ministers, and long-suffering spouses had been unable to break the downward spiral, but suddenly it was done — through the love of one drunk for another. In the act of helping another person, the impulses were muted. Craving gave in to serenity. An incurable disease had met its master: love.

Anyone can love. It doesn't take brains. It doesn't take looks. It doesn't take wealth, social status, training, breeding, education, muscular coordination, alertness, quickness, concentration, psychic ability, or any other credentials. "Love, and do what you will," said St. Augustine.

In the throes of our addiction, love had been a stranger. Some of us couldn't recognize it. We were sure that if it existed, it had long passed us by. But love is never a stranger to any of us.

"Altruism has always been one of biology's deep mysteries," says biologist Lewis Thomas in his book of essays, *Late Night Thoughts on Listening to Mahler's Ninth Symphony*.

> Why should any animal, off on its own, specified and labeled by all sorts of signals as its individual self, choose to give up its life in aid of someone else? . . . At first glance, it seems an unnatural act, a violation of nature, to give away one's life, or even one's possessions, to another. And yet, in the face of improbability, examples of altruism abound. . . . I maintain, despite the moment's evidence against the claim, that we are born and grow up with a fondness for each other, and we have genes for that. We can be talked out of it, for the genetic message is like a distant music and some of us are hard-of-hearing. Societies are noisy affairs, drowning out the sound of ourselves and our connection. Hard-of-hearing, we go to war. Stone-deaf, we make thermonuclear missiles. Nonetheless, the music is there, waiting for more listeners.[1]

---

[1] Thomas, Lewis, *Late Night Thoughts on Listening to Mahler's Ninth Symphony* (New York: Viking Press, 1984), 101, 105.

"The music" is there, too, even in the midst of war. Glenn J. Gray, an American professor of philosophy who spent part of World War II interviewing captured enemy soldiers on the battlefields of Europe, considered the phenomenon in his book, *The Warriors: Reflections on Men in Battle.*

> Numberless soldiers have died, more or less
> willingly not for country or honor or religious faith or
> for any other abstract good, but because they realized
> that by fleeing their post and rescuing themselves, they
> would expose their companions to greater danger.[2]

Altruism. Another name for love?

Dr. Lewis Thomas is an evolutionist and might not like to be identified with anything such as a spiritual cousinhood. But the "distant music" he speaks of in his essay on altruism is heard in another dimension. Listen to it described in *A Course in Miracles:*

> Listen — perhaps you catch a hint of an ancient
> state not quite forgotten; dim, perhaps, and yet not
> altogether unfamiliar, like a song whose name is long
> forgotten, and the circumstances in which you heard
> completely unremembered. Not the whole song has
> stayed with you, but just a little wisp of melody,
> attached not to a person or a place or anything
> particular. But you remember, from just this little part,
> how lovely was the song, how wonderful the setting
> where you heard it, and how you loved those who
> were there and listened with you.
> The notes are nothing. Yet you have kept them with
> you, not for themselves, but as a soft reminder of what
> would make you weep if you remembered how dear it
> was to you. You could remember, yet you are afraid,

------

[2]   Gray, Glenn, J. *The Warriors: Reflections on Men in Battle*

believing you would lose the world you learned since then. And yet you know that nothing in the world you learned is half so dear as this. Listen, and see if you remember an ancient song you knew so long ago and held more dear than any melody you taught yourself to cherish since.

Beyond the body, beyond the sun and stars, past everything you see and yet somehow familiar, is an arc of golden light that stretches as you look into a great and shining circle. And all the circle fills with light before your eyes. The edges of the circle disappear, and what is in it is no longer contained at all. The light expands and covers everything, extending to infinity forever shining and with no break or limit anywhere. Within it everything is joined in perfect continuity. Nor is it possible to imagine that anything could be outside, for there is nowhere that this light is not.

. . . Here is the memory of what you are; a part of this, with all of it within, and joined to all as surely as all is joined in you.[3]

Dr. Thomas talks of the music of altruism, "a fondness for each other," buried in our genes. *A Course in Miracles* sings a mystic refrain, evoking the memory of an ancient melody and of a light beyond the stars. Are not both tracing a common ancestry whose linkage is love?

What if they're right? Every time we resist love, every time we block it, deflect it, dodge it, withhold it — we're committing an unnatural act! "Your task is not to seek for love, but merely to seek and find all of the barriers within yourself that you have built against it," says *A Course in Miracles*.

---

[3] *A Course in Miracles* (Tiburon, Calif.: Foundation for Inner Peace, Inc., 1975), vol. 1, 416, 417. (Portions) Reprinted by Permission from *A Course in Miracles* © Copyright 1975, Foundation for Inner Peace, Inc.

"The truth is revealed," says Alan Watts in *The Wisdom of Insecurity* "by removing things that stand in its light, an art not unlike sculpture, in which the artist creates, not by building, but by hacking away."[4]

When we give in to love, when we remove the barriers to love and surrender to it, we are back home where we're supposed to be. We are who we're supposed to be.

---

[4] Watts, Alan, *The Wisdom of Insecurity* (New York: Pantheon Books, 1951), 77.

TURN IT OVER

Man is a technically misbegotten creature, half finished and ill equipped, but in his mind and soul are all the ingredients of a creator, of an artist.

— *Eric Hoffer in*
Eric Hoffer, An American Odyssey

We're now entering the Land of Spiritual Growth. But beware. This is rough territory. The trail that winds through this unexplored landscape is booby-trapped.

"Made a decision to turn our will and our lives over to the care of God *as we understood Him.*"

The Mighty Ego conducts guerrilla warfare here. Its favorite expression is "made a decision," because it knows how long self-improvement decisions last. The Mighty Ego knows a common complaint of recovering addicts is this: "I turn it over, but I keep taking it back."

Don't be fooled. It is not you, not the spiritual you taking it back. It is the one and only Mighty Ego doing this. Although it professes to be your friend, and is in fact your inseparable companion, this personality is really your dedicated enemy. The Mighty Ego, which is a creation of your own mind — a body of thought, a lifelong accumulation of selfish ideas energized by your glands, your animal instincts, and years of bad advice — is shocked that you would seek counsel from anything other than itself.

The Mighty Ego is sure it is the font of all wisdom. And why not? We've given it every reason to think so; we've often relied on its judgment.

The Mighty Ego is the ultimate in self-centeredness. It is familiar with the concept of God, but it has no use for God except as a standard against which it can measure its own exalted sense of worth. Because of God's reputation for power and wisdom, the

Ego at least considers God a worthy opponent. But not an equal. It considers God inferior, and with good reason: we have nearly always consulted it rather than God. Too often we have done what the Ego wants; we have not thought to ask what God wants.

The Mighty Ego can't believe we are now shifting allegiance. It will do everything in its power to retain control and to thwart us. And its power — the power that we have given it over a lifetime — is considerable.

Didn't it show us the way out of our fears by talking us into our addiction?

Didn't it make us compulsive and subservient?

Didn't it eventually terrify us?

Didn't it then offer us the means and the motives for our death?

The Mighty Ego is not afraid of death; it is sure that it lives independent of us and would live on. It considers it a bother to be entangled with us. It wants out! And so it doesn't hesitate to make us think we're sick and weak if we don't listen to it.

Ever since I started exploring the Eleventh Step in earnest, my own Mighty Ego has had a go at putting me down every now and then. It nearly always attacks when I've had a particularly meaningful contact with God as I understand Him, when I've been blessed with a new spiritual insight. Suddenly, swoosh goes the wind out of my sails. This has happened so often at times of spiritual growth that I have come to expect it.

But for the Mighty Ego, it's a losing battle. Once a decision for God has been made, it is irreversible. The spiritual part of us has come to that decision and will not change it. The only inner guide that we can trust now is at work.

Many of us make contact with that guide at the hardest time in our life. When we reach the point of utter futility, the place at which we have lost all hope (as most addicts eventually do), we become spiritually teachable.

Groping our way through a dark night of despair, each of us comes to a place where we are forced to make a decision about our lives. Those of us who ask for help, choosing the path of spiritual growth, never turn back.

We do take our wills back, of course, all the time. The Mighty Ego delights in this, causes it, and loves to see us distracted. But we cannot take back the decision. A spiritual commitment does change us forever.

I've lost count of the times I've given up, feeling again, as I have so many times before, that I am not cut out for the spiritual life — that I am too self-centered, too vain, too concerned with my physical and material desires, and have said to hell with it, only to find myself, a day or two later, avidly poring over some of the writings that speak to me, rejoicing in some new insight, praying for more enlightenment.

My Higher Power does not let go. The first time I made the decision, He took me at my word, and He is holding me to it. But the Ego is vigilant. It tries to capture control at every opportunity. The slightest distraction and it's back in charge.

Every time we realize the Mighty Ego has taken over again, we have an opportunity to get back in touch with our Higher Power. The decision to turn our will and our life over to the care of God as we understand Him was the smartest thing we ever did. And the need to keep rededicating ourselves to that principle is a blessing, not a curse.

Keeping Contact With Our Higher Power

Many recovering people working Twelve Step programs try to make a point of getting in touch with their Higher Power the first thing in the morning and the last thing at night. But prayer and meditation can be done any time we need guidance. It doesn't hurt to renew our decision, and to do it as often as it takes to keep our eyes on our recovery.

My friend, Ray, in New Mexico revealed the other day that he had "made the astonishing discovery, almost nineteen years after beginning these anonymous programs, that I have permission to work the Third Step *every minute of the day*."

There is no limit to the number of times we can make a decision to turn our life and our will over to the care of God as we understand Him. And every time we do it, we draw closer to His will. For me, that decision is reaffirmed every time I ask for help.

"God, help me in dealing with this person."

"Holy friend, show me what to do here."

"I can't handle this situation, Lord. Give me the words to say."

James, an alcoholic San Francisco college professor posed this question at an A.A. meeting:

"What if before I had breakfast in the morning I asked God to guide me in terms of what I was going to eat? You see, I don't do that. Suppose I did? Or what I was going to wear? Or what I was going to say to the next person I met?

"All of these kinds of conditioned things that I do, really without giving them a lot of thought . . . what if? What if in one day, just one twenty-four-hour period, before I did any single thing, I asked God to guide me in my thoughts, my words, and my actions? What if I did that? What would the effect be? I don't know because I've never really tried it."

James said he'd read in Emmet Fox's *Sermon on the Mount* that this is exactly what Moses did. For every single thing he did, before he did it, he would ask God, "What should I do?" And that, according to A.A., is what humility is: the recognition of the presence of God in every aspect of our lives.

"Now think about it," James said, caught up in the excitement of his idea. "What if I were God? Wouldn't I be rather pleased if one of my creations talked to me about what he or she was going to do in the same sense that I might talk to a parent or a loved one about some decision I was about to make?

"What if," James asked, "I paid that much attention to God? What if I thought so much of God in my life that I actually recognized Him in the same way that I do my wife, and I said, 'God, Kathy and I have talked about this and I would like to get your input on it.' What if?"

"I know," answered Rick, another A.A. member. "I'd like to be able to remember to ask for guidance in everything I do, too, and of course I don't do that either." Some of us smiled to ourselves. Rick is a surgeon. And at one time his hand was none too steady. He's fine now. But even so, what if? What if he asked for divine guidance before each incision?

"One thing I do, though," Rick said, "when I think of it (and as time goes along I'm thinking of it more and more) is that whenever I have any kind of a meeting coming up with somebody, an encounter of some kind, I will quickly ask my Higher Power to handle this with me.

"And it just works beautifully. It always works. And not the way I would have it work either. He makes it work for everybody concerned. I can be meeting somebody that I really resent, and if I ask for help for this particular relationship, it doesn't just work out for me, it works out for this person that I'm angry with too. God doesn't play favorites."

Some people call these coincidences. How can we really know what happens in situations like that? Just a naive confidence, born of a shaky faith, might be enough to change one's attitude going into a difficult encounter. One person having a relaxed, helpful attitude might be enough to jog the others into letting down their guards. Just a smile might do it. And when the tension goes out of a meeting, anything can happen, usually something good for everyone involved. So, some say, don't go around chalking everything up to some unseen power.

Okay, good point. But recovering addicts working their Twelve Step programs, and many other people, have reason to wonder why they keep noticing so many coincidences, if that's what they are. Some call them miracles. The appearance of serendipity in our lives is habit-forming. We almost take it for granted. But we have learned to be grateful.

Still, there's room for doubt. "In fact," says Leo, who owns a haberdashery, "doubt is a necessary element of faith. For faith without doubt is . . . knowledge."

Knowledge has been a handicap for many of us. We knew it all. Our towering intellects had been capable of solving all the mysteries of the universe. All except one: the mystery of how a simple substance, a simple habit, a physical impulse, a mental fixation, could enslave us and why we couldn't master it with our minds.

I think if I were capable of true knowledge, in the realm of the spirit, it would be that we — all of us — are already in the care of God, no matter what we have decided for ourselves. Isn't it possible that in the Third Step what we are really deciding to do is give up the idea that we are on our own? In making our decision, and renewing it as often as seems needed, aren't we really only acknowledging that we had never left the protection of God in the first place?

It makes sense to me that our will is already God's will. Unfortunately, we don't usually recognize it as such. Instead, we see a conflict between what we want God's will to be and what it actually is. Or so we think.

"It's been a struggle over the years," says Pat, a retired civil service worker. "I've always thought very highly of myself and my mental capacity. It's been difficult, but slowly and surely I think I'm reaching the point where I feel comfortable recognizing that I can't go through this life on my own willpower."

"I had been running on Sam power for most of my life," said an alcoholic named Sam. "My own willpower. And that is finite. It ran out. My power always runs out. But God's power never, never runs out."

God's will and God's power are there for all of us, and we can experience it simply by acknowledging it. They're at our instant disposal, and all we have to do to activate them is to make our daily or hourly or minute-by-minute decision to let Him guide us. All we have to do is get in touch and thereby acknowledge that we are not alone. Whatever we do thereafter, it seems to me, has got to be the will of God, whether it feels like it or not.

Trying to understand this power is beyond humankind's intellectual capacity. To match my wits with God is to come off looking utterly stupid. To challenge Him is to emphasize my helplessness.

Coming Back Home

I have a pair of cockatiels that like to assert their independence. When let out of their cage, they don't ask where in the house they can fly — they just take off. They don't ask my permission or for an itinerary — they just wing it. And the birds at first don't appreciate my trying to coax them back to the cage. They squawk and fuss, and peck my hand. But after awhile, when they grow tired of their freedom and want food and water, they ride a finger back to their home. It's really the only place they feel secure.

At that point my will is their will. And at some comparable point in my own flights of fancy, God's will is mine. I need to keep being brought back home.

When I fly out on the wings of the Mighty Ego, I am insufferably arrogant and painfully independent. I, too, peck at the hand that feeds me. My intellect is all that I think I need. But my power goes only so far. Soon I'm clinging to the hand of God, who knows where my home is. He will take me there and feed me, welcoming me back to my will and His.

I am always free to fly where I wish. I am also free to consult with my Higher Power before taking off. When I train myself to make my decisions with Him, when I begin to get in the habit of doing that, my relationships improve. My frustrations level off. My life works.

APPRECIATION

*The mark of your ignorance is the depth of your
belief in injustice and tragedy.*

> — *Richard Bach*
> Illusions

It would seem that the most natural way for us to view someone is critically. Upon encountering anyone, friend or stranger, that's what most of us do. We judge and evaluate. We mentally criticize. We find fault. We don't have to do that. We can train our mind to look at everyone in a different way, a nonjudgmental way.

Johnny, a housebuilder from Kansas, made a big impression on me when I first got sober. He had about seventeen years of sobriety at that time, and the first thing I noticed about him when he addressed the group, other than his red hair, was that he had the kindest eyes I had ever seen. And he looked right at me when, unbelievably, he said: "I am grateful for what God has given me — through you."

I think of Johnny when I try to do as he did — look at everyone with appreciation. That's the attitude that best helps me deal with people. Regardless of what someone is doing, or has done, I can view that person with appreciation.

It's amazing how this attitude changes my feelings toward people. I find myself feeling good about the kinds of people I used to despise. And I now know how self-defeating it was to despise them.

My judgment of someone is invariably faulty. I don't know anyone well enough to judge him or her.

This is how it's put in *A Course in Miracles:*

> In order to judge anything rightly one would have to
> be fully aware of an inconceivably wide range of
> things — past, present, and to come. One would have

51

to recognize in advance all the effects of his judgments on everyone and everything involved with them in any way. And one would have to be certain there is no distortion in his perception, so that his judgment would be wholly fair to everyone on whom it rests now and in the future. Who is in a position to do this?[1].

Not I. If someone seems to me to be an angel or a devil, it matters not. My judgment is bound to be wrong. I can count on it. What helps me — and the person — is just to show appreciation.

I don't have to approve of what someone is doing, but I need to approve of the person. I need to appreciate him or her. If I do that, regardless of who it is or what the person is doing, it helps remind me that there are certain things that others can do, which are okay for them, that I cannot do because they are bad for me.

For example, I don't think lying helps anyone. But I cannot look down on someone for lying. If someone lies to me, it may affect our relationship. But that's his or her responsibility. I've done my share of lying and suffered the consequences. It's not healthy for me to be part of anyone else's consequences. I have enough of a job handling my own.

I can disapprove of what a person is doing without losing appreciation of him or her. Yet, even if I say I disapprove of someone's behavior only in relation to what it does to me, I have to be careful. I need to understand my motives. I shouldn't disapprove in a smug, condescending way. Who am I to look down my nose at anybody?

If I don't like what someone is doing, I need to look at it as something that may be okay for that person to do, and perhaps even inevitable for the person to be doing it at his or her level of spiritual growth, but perhaps not necessarily okay for me at my level.

---

[1] *A Course In Miracles* (Tiburon, Calif.: Foundation for Inner Peace, 1975), vol. 3, 26. Reprinted with permission.

And yet, without even realizing it, look what I've just done. How patronizing what I just wrote sounds, and how patronizing it is. As soon as I started thinking about "levels of growth," I began comparing myself to another and fell into an ego trap that allowed me to look down on that person and demonstrate how superior I am.

The instant that I judge my behavior or my reasoning ability as superior to someone else's, I have lost my ability to experience that person as an equal. That the other person is my equal is always true, no matter what I think.

What I choose to see in others, I'm really seeing in myself. It is inescapable. Again, from *A Course in Miracles:*

> Teach no one that he is what you would not want to be. Your brother is the mirror in which you see the image of yourself.[2]

If I can avoid the ego trap of assessing someone's behavior, I have an opportunity to grow. In fact, if I work it right, every encounter with someone is an opportunity to grow. In everything I do, I am host to my Higher Power or hostage to my ego. One is liberating; the other enslaving.

I owe appreciation to everyone regardless of what he or she is doing because everyone is an opportunity for me. If the person is expressing love, I can share in the happiness and joy of that moment. If it is not love, it is a call for help. Anger, spite, insensitivity — it doesn't matter. All nonloving expressions are calls for help. And I can help myself only by answering those calls with help.

And with love and appreciation.

---

[2] *A Course In Miracles,* vol. 1, 118. Reprinted with permission.

DIALOGUE WITH MYSELF

What I want from God I must be prepared to give to others. That's how I get it.

What do I want from God?

Peace.

Then it must be peace that I give to others.

Yes.

How do I give peace to others?

By giving them no reason for distress. No judgment. No condemnation. Not the slightest hint. Give them only appreciation.

Is that possible for someone as judgmental as I am?

Probably not, by yourself.

If it's useless, why then should I even try?

It is not useless. Ask for the power from the Source of all power.

Okay. And how do I offer peace?

By showing appreciation.

How can I show appreciation when I am so full of criticism and judgment?

Again, ask for the power. And appreciate it when it comes. For it surely will come.

What if I just don't notice it? My prayers aren't always answered.

Prayers seldom are answered in a vacuum. There is a surer way. Put your arm around friends or acquaintances, or give them a pat, or just a smile. Encourage them; pick out something to praise. Look for something specific that's worth a good word, then say it. See what happens: God will smile back. A feeling of peace will come over you. Feel the beauty, and appreciate it.

ASK

But seriously, is not man a miserable creature?
Scarcely does he come into his own powers naturally,
to taste a complete, entire and pure pleasure, but that
he sets out to curtail it by reasoning. Not wretched
enough, he adds to his misery by art and study.

— *Michel de Montaigne*

Appreciating everyone I meet is rarely easy to do. It's one thing to know that I can improve my relationships by showing appreciation for each person, but it's something else to do it. I can't command myself to appreciate someone and expect it to automatically happen. My mind is not a computer. I cannot punch a key marked "A" on my mental keyboard and show appreciation.

It's much easier to classify things and feelings than it is to produce them. When I have combined the feelings of approval, admiration, happiness, and support (not to mention a few other shades of emotion), what I have produced is a symbol called appreciation — not the thing itself. I have produced a word that stands for what I feel. This ability is one of humankind's most remarkable achievements. Forming thoughts about the things we see and feel, and matching them with symbols and sounds in a complex system of communication has moved humanity to do many great things, all the way to building rocket ships to carry us to the moon. Unfortunately, this ability — the ability to express ourselves abstractly — also carried us away from our real self, our spiritual self.

In prehistoric times, the matching of words and ideas with the sounds we brought forth from our throat was a source of wonder. It also made our world efficient. It saved both time and energy for the tired hunter to say "give — me — water" than to bring his mate down to the stream and point at the gourd that he wanted her to fill and bring back to the cave.

This worked well for us early humans for a while, but then we began to confuse the sounds, the words, the symbols with the real thing. Words are a convenience, just as money is. Money allows us to trade something of value for something else of value. Instead of lugging around a ham and looking for someone who has a bushel of grain, we trade coin and paper, although we know the coin and paper are basically worthless. Words, too, are basically worthless without the ideas they express.

When early humans were learning to speak, words must have seemed magical, possessing an awesome power. They effortlessly expressed our fondest wishes and summoned the things we desired. The words we used to refer to ourselves took on special meaning. We used words like "I," "me," and our own names to define us and distinguish ourselves from other people.

Through language we came to know ourselves as individuals, but we lost our tribal identity — our feeling of being a part of a whole — when we began to think of ourselves as different. Carried to the extreme, the experience of being different from others can set us apart so that we feel isolated, cut off from everyone and everything, including our Higher Power.

An old Army colonel friend of mine says he came into A.A. not believing much of anything about how he came to be. "I got to thinking, though, that there can't be any such thing as an atheist. If there is, he's got to prove to somebody that he created himself. And every time I went to do that I had a hell of a time."

This friend still isn't buying anybody's theology, but he has something he's comfortable with. "After thirteen years in the program," he says, "I have had what I call a spiritual awakening. I found out about love — the love that one person has for another — also the belief that I'm not an individual, but that I am part of a large organism. The better I conduct myself, the better the organism conducts itself."

That's a profound leap of faith and an expression of deepest appreciation of one's fellows. Today, when I consciously try to appreciate other people, it's not so easy to do; thinking the word may not summon the feeling.

That's when I have to ask my Higher Power for help. Asking for help in each encounter is what summons this feeling of appreciation. That it is given me by my Higher Power I have little doubt. Asking for help when I meet a brother or sister blesses our relationship and returns us to the larger world of Spirit.

ONE SPIRIT

And I know that the spirit of God is the brother of
my own,
And that all the men ever born are also my brothers.

— Walt Whitman

If I had been entirely able to do without other people, I would have done so. Come to think of it, I did try. I used my drinking to shut people out. I always felt that I was on the outside looking in, never quite able to feel comfortable with people or to relate to them — parents, brothers, teachers, schoolmates, barracks mates, wives, children, bosses, or fellow workers. There was a constant awareness of separation, of not belonging.

Now I feel just the opposite. I do belong. And all of the people in my life are not just people I belong with but people I must be with to be whole. I look upon most of them as friends and all as brothers and sisters.

What brought about the change? It started, of course, with defeat and surrender. When I honestly acknowledged that I desperately needed help, I received it — not from my confused mind, not from the judgmental God of my childhood, but from a loving and kind Higher Power and from people just like me. Afterward, I began to feel a part of the people around me, that I did belong.

It was slow in coming. Thinking back, I guess I had never really trusted other people. I was a loner, as independent as they come. I was sure that I could understand anything I put my mind to, and could solve all problems. Yet I was terrified of people, places, and things — a paradox that I daily sought to drown in vodka.

Now I see I can't do without the fellow inhabitants of this planet. When my Higher Power gets in touch with me, or when I quietly listen, i feel peaceful and very much a part of what is happening around me. This often happens at Twelve Step meetings. It also happens increasingly at home or work. Someone says something, quite innocently, and it comes to me that it is no coincidence, no accident that I am where I am.

I enjoy being with family, friends, acquaintances, and strangers. Being with other people is the only way I know to get out of myself. Time spent in isolation fretting over things I can't control is wasted time. It only makes me nervous and miserable. But time spent with others — listening, encouraging, sharing their happiness, their accomplishments, concerns, and sadness — is satisfying time. It feels good.

"I do believe you have to get other-directed," says Kathleen, a fifteen-year veteran of A.A. "If I'm going through a self-centered period, then my responsibility is to get other-directed. The only way I can do that is with the help of God. I've found out that by myself I'm not able to get out of myself. I tend to get in the way."

We will never be entirely selfless, of course. The very act of turning our attention to others is selfish in a way, since it is through others that we gain everything of value. *A Course in Miracles* says:

> When you meet anyone, remember it is a holy encounter. As you treat him you will treat yourself. As you think of him you will think of yourself. Never forget this, for in him you will find yourself or lose yourself.[1]

The New Testament says:

> He that saith he is in the light and hateth his brother is in darkness . . . he that loveth his brother abideth in the light.[2]

---

[1] *A Course In Miracles*, vol. 1, 132. Reprinted with permission.
[2] John 2:9.

These are not meaningless platitudes. They are tried and true. We need to pay close attention to how we treat the people around us. And then we need to think how it makes us feel, honestly.

Again, from *A Course in Miracles:*

> It is not up to you to change your brother but
> merely to accept him as he is.[3]

With my ego screaming at me that somebody's got to tell the jerk how wrong he is, this is not the easiest piece of advice I ever received. When we try to accept people as they are, something happens. A weight is lifted. The "brother" the Bible and *A Course in Miracles* are talking about is the guy at the office, my best friend, my wife, and (oh Lord!) my kids. I have to swallow a lot of pride, but once I make the effort to accept them as they are, little by little, they begin to be nicer people. Try it and see what happens to the people around you. It might be interesting.

"Your brother is as right as you are," says *A Course in Miracles,* "and if you think he is wrong, you are condemning yourself."[4]

We no longer feel responsible for determining what is good and bad in each person. We recognize that's not our call.

Everything in us rebels against that. All of us can recall when our friends, co-workers, acquaintances, and family members have been and still are in the wrong. We can cite chapter and verse. But can we handle being the judge?

Twelve Steps and Twelve Traditions reminds us of this:

> It is a spiritual axiom that every time we are
> disturbed, no matter what the cause, there is
> something wrong *with us.*[5]

---

[3] *A Course in Miracles,* vol. 1, 156. Reprinted with permission.
[4] *A Course in Miracles,* vol. 1, 156. Reprinted with permission.
[5] *Twelve Steps and Twelve Traditions* (New York: A.A. World Services, Inc., 1964), 92.

If we are annoyed, angry, embarrassed, or disgusted, it is often because we have not measured up to our standards or are reacting to something someone did or said. We have to remind ourselves that we are responsible for our feelings.

"I believe that quote from Lincoln that's in the Big Book," said George, a red-headed Irishman. "It says most people are about as happy as they make up their minds to be. I think that's true. But the problem I have as an alcoholic is how do I make up my mind to be something I haven't been? I think achieving that attitude change comes from a reliance on God. When I turn my life and my will over to the power of God, as I understand Him, then the attitude change occurs."

Two Things We Can Depend On

1. Other people change. So do we. No one will be quite the same today as yesterday.
2. Spiritual principles we have learned to depend on never change.

Other people's actions are theirs. Our reactions are our own. One need not have anything to do with the other. What's more, it's dangerous for us to let our balance hinge on what someone else does or says. As addicts, we can't afford it.

"If somebody hurts us and we are sore, we are in the wrong also," says the *Twelve by Twelve*. "But are there no exceptions to this rule? What about 'justifiable' anger? If somebody cheats us, aren't we entitled to be mad? Can't we be properly angry with self-righteous people? For us of A.A. these are dangerous exceptions. We have found that justified anger ought to be left to those better qualified to handle it."[6]

Likewise, we can't expect other people's balance to hinge on what we say or do. We need to be loving, considerate, respectful, and we need to examine the motives for the things we do.

---

[6] *Twelve Steps and Twelve Traditions*, 92.

Are we trying to win a useless argument? Are we sure we aren't criticizing someone just to feel superior? Are we trying to teach a lesson or to punish?

All too often my motivations in dealing with others are self-centered. And I'm not sure I can do anything about that on my own. I have to have help. My obsession with getting my own way is not going to vanish by wishing it away. My Higher Power wants me to get out and work this out with people.

The people around me and I are one. And if I am to find my way in this world, all the things I ask for myself I must be willing to give to others, including the benefit of the doubt.

Somebody said this:

> *I sought my soul, and it escaped me.*
> *I sought my God and He eluded me.*
> *I sought my brother, and found all three.*

I have to practice trusting others. If I don't, I'll miss something I need to hear . . . as well as the whole point of being here.

DEFENSELESSNESS

So long as man resists a situation, he will have it with him. If he runs away from it, it will run after him.

— *Florence S. Shinn*
The Game of Life and How to Play It

A hindrance to spiritual progress is my habit of defending myself against all comers. Even when the spirit of brotherhood seems to be pulsing in my veins, it is hard to get over the feeling that it's me against the world, and if I don't defend myself, who will?

No matter how much I may love others, no matter how determined I may be to get along with them, conflicts happen. They are unavoidable. The clash of wills, even between the best of friends, is as old as Cain and Abel.

My Higher Power may have removed my compulsion to drink, but He didn't remove my free will. I can still choose to drink, just as I can choose to lie, cheat, steal, and fight with my neighbors. But if we're to advance along a spiritual path, our goal must be to get along with as many of the people we meet as possible, even those we dislike. We claim spiritual progress rather than spiritual perfection.

Jesus' advice to "agree with thine adversary quickly" doesn't necessarily mean we have to always agree with everyone, but at least we can agree that it's okay to have differences of opinion. We don't have to be upset and hold on to our feelings of resistance. The disagreement will only worsen.

We can't afford to resist everything other people do or say, any more than we can afford to resist our feelings. Resistance turns into resentment, and that's unhealthy, dangerous stuff. Better to shift gears and replace our antagonistic thoughts with something else. We can learn to choose the thoughts we act on.

June, a single mother and a recovering drug addict, says she has a temper but that she can't quit fighting with people just because she wants to. "I can't just give up my character defects; I have to replace them with other behaviors."

Slow-talking Joe, an ex-con, says he learned to replace his fighting thoughts with prayer. "I got so I was willing to work on my anger and my resentment, willing to make an effort to overcome them. That's where God came in. I had to do a lot of praying when these things would come up."

If I don't like what I'm thinking and feeling, I have to replace them with other thoughts and feelings; fighting them only makes the conflict worse. Asking God to guide my thoughts is the surest way to stop the fighting.

A Course in Miracles says:

> In my defenselessness my safety lies. You who feel
> threatened by this changing world, its twists of fortune
> and its bitter jests, its brief relationships and all the
> 'gifts' it merely lends to take away again; attend this
> lesson well. The world provides no safety . . . the
> world gives rise but to defensiveness.[1]

Alan W. Watts, in his book, *Nature, Man and Woman,* pointed out that psychological defenses against suffering are futile.

> The more we defend, the more we suffer. And
> defending is itself suffering. Although we cannot help
> putting up the psychological defense, it dissolves when
> it is seen that the defense is all of a piece with what we
> are defending ourselves against.[2]

We couldn't quit drinking as long as we resisted the fact that we were powerless over alcohol and that we needed help. We

---

[1] *A Course In Miracles*, vol. 2, 277. Reprinted with permission.
[2] Watts, Alan A., *Nature, Man and Woman* (New York: Pantheon Books Inc., 1958), 92.

were in terror of what our disease was doing to us but we feared even more giving up control of our lives. It wasn't until we surrendered, an action we thought to be the epitome of weakness, that some control was returned to us.

The Key to Our Mental Health: Drop Our Defenses

We are children of God, and what is there about a child of God that needs defending? People are not a threat to us if we have nothing that needs protection from them. Our most important attribute is love and that is something we share with everyone.

Each of us wants the freedom to love. And we can have that freedom if we break down the barriers of fear — whether anger, envy, or greed — we have built.

By fearing what other people think and feel, we deepen their resolve to defend themselves. We convince them that their position must be defended — that their soul depends on it. And we convince ourselves that it is important, that our own soul depends on pointing out their error. But by doing this, we don't correct their error; we join them in it. Their error is to believe that what they are asserting is what really matters; our error is to believe that correcting them is what really matters. Neither of us will get anything out of it but anger and fear.

What if we were to adopt the attitude that we can't correct other people, that only God can do that?

What if we were to believe that the only thing other people need from us is love?

I worked in almost perpetual conflict with an older man for about four years. We were both strong-minded. Right from the start we took our disagreements personally. It got so that all we had to do is take one look at each other and our shields went up and our swords came out. How dare he question my authority? How dare I question his greater experience and sharper mind? One day I had enough. I called him into my office and said, "George, you and I have had hard feelings about each other for a long time. It's affecting my peace of mind and the quality of my work, and I imagine it's affecting yours."

Then I took a deep breath and said what I had already decided would be one of the hardest things I'd ever have to say. I was scared. I didn't know how he would take it. I didn't know how it would make me look.

"I want you to know that it's my fault. And from now on, I'm going to try to be more pleasant."

George was dumbfounded. Tears came to his eyes and he mumbled something to the effect that he was just as much at fault. We had many disagreements after that. But none of them were ever bitter again. Our relationship was transformed overnight into one of mutual respect and affection. Notice that I didn't tell him that I had been wrong in my disagreements with him; I was simply wrong in my attitude toward him, in the way I had treated him. I dropped my shield and handed him my sword. That's what patched things up, along with hearing from me that I cared enough about him to put my pride on the line.

The only sane response to conflict is love. We can accept that disagreements can't always be avoided. But in doing that we also need to believe that differences of opinion don't have to interfere with love. They are not a threat unless we give them that power.

When we look upon conflict as a threat and try to defend ourselves, we ensure fear. When we ask for help and turn it over to our Higher Power, the conflict is resolved. And we are free to love others once again.

Defensiveness takes other forms too. How many times, for example, have we rehearsed what we were going to say to our boss or to our spouse or to fellow A.A.'s — only to have the words vanish when summoned? Our defenses usually crumble at the crucial moment.

What if we were to consciously drop our guard each time we approach a person or a situation that makes us nervous?

What if we were to practice repeating to ourselves, *In my defenselessness my safety lies* every time a difficult encounter arose?

We might discover a new calmness when we can practice defenselessness and depend on our Higher Power to supply the words.

FORGIVENESS

It is by forgiving that one is forgiven.

— *St. Francis of Assisi*

"Acceptance of oneself is the essence of the moral problem and the acid test of one's whole outlook on life," said Carl Jung, the renowned Swiss psychologist, talking to a group of ministers in 1932. Jung also said:

> That I feed the beggar, that I forgive an insult, that I love my enemy in the name of Christ — all these are undoubtedly great virtues. What I do unto the least of my brethren, that I do unto Christ. But what if I should discover that the least amongst them all, the poorest of all beggars, the most impudent of all offenders, yea the very fiend himself — these are within me, and that I myself stand in the need of the alms of my own kindness, that I myself am the enemy who must be loved — what then?

Is it possible that we despise some people because they are as unworthy and unattractive as we imagine ourselves to be? Is it possible that we fear others because we suspect they are too much like the worst in ourselves — critical, vindictive, uncompromising, unforgiving?

Here's Montaigne quoting Plato:

> If I find a thing unsound, is it not because I am myself unsound? Am I not myself at fault? May not my observations reflect upon myself?

And Montaigne, in his own words:

> Our eyes can see nothing behind us. A hundred times a day we laugh at ourselves when we laugh at

our neighbors; and we detest in others the faults which
are much more glaring in ourselves.

If what we ridicule and fear most in others are our faults, why
can't we forgive ourselves and be done with it? By doing so,
might everyone else be automatically absolved of guilt?

For some reason it doesn't seem to work that way. We may
see our shortcomings in others so that each is in some way a mir-
ror of ourselves. But when we forgive ourselves or say we do,
we often still see those glaring defects as belonging to others.
What are we doing wrong?

It may be that we're playing God when we think we're
qualified to judge what our sins are or spot defects in others.

"I really don't want to do that anymore," says Kathleen, who
at the age of seventeen came out of an alcoholic blackout to find
herself bludgeoning a girlfriend half to death with a telephone.
"I can't tell you how to live or how not to live. I don't want the
responsibility. I'm very happy to turn you over to God." It has
become vital for Kathleen in fifteen years of sober living not to
take anybody else's inventory.

How ironic it is that our Higher Power seems to speak clearest
to us through the very people whose defects we're so intent on
correcting. If we're busy finding fault in others, we may miss out
on something important. Our only hope is not to look for errors
in others, but to keep an open mind.

"You can only know God through an open mind, just as you
can only see the sky through a clear window," said Alan Watts.
"You will not see the sky if you have covered the glass with blue
paint."[1] By the same token, we need to stop coloring other
people with our ego's judgment.

My copy of *A Course in Miracles* has a defect in the binding that
causes it to fall open each time to the page that bears these words:

---

[1] Watts, Alan A. *The Wisdom of Insecurity* (New York: Pantheon Books,
1951), 25.

Those who remember always that they know nothing, and who have become willing to learn everything, will learn it. But whenever they trust themselves, they will not learn. . . . Whenever you think you know, peace will depart from you, because you have abandoned the Teacher of peace. Whenever you fully realize that you know not, peace will return, for you will have invited Him to do so by abandoning the ego on behalf of Him.[2]

It's Okay to Say, "I Don't Know"

We can actually take comfort in our ignorance in that we don't know what to forgive in ourselves or in others. Something we see as a character defect may be a source of help to someone else. We need to get out of the habit of correcting other people's errors, step back and let our Higher Power handle it.

And we need to practice humility even in the act of forgiveness. Something as basic as forgiveness has pitfalls for us.

We can use forgiveness as a way to puff up our ego so that it becomes an opportunity to see what's wrong with other people and, ever so generously, not hold it against them. We may say that God created us equal, but when we sit as the judge while forgiving, we set ourselves up as superior to others and separate ourselves from them.

Forgiveness can seem so hard that we may try and make do with something a little safer like acceptance: "I accept you just as you are."

Yet it's forgiveness that speaks to our deepest needs. True forgiveness is an act of love, and only love overlooks errors. In fact, it doesn't see them at all. From love's point of view, nothing ever needed correcting. All is forgiven without a thought.

---

[2] *A Course In Miracles*, vol. 1, 278. Reprinted with permission.

But aren't there things people have done to us that we just can't let go of? Things that we believe are unforgivable? How does one forgive the unforgivable?

"I've got to be able to forgive," says Jersey John. "If I can't forgive, I can kiss serenity good-bye."

And what we can't do our Higher Power can do for us. Thank goodness pardon is always possible with my Higher Power, for haven't I done things that many people would consider unforgivable? What addict hasn't had the same thought?

The God of my understanding saw my behavior as an outgrowth of distress. My errors came from fear and confusion that grew out of alienation from my Higher Power. Is that a pardonable offense? If God is love, yes.

Our goal becomes to offer others the forgiveness God offers us. This is how we can demonstrate true compassion to someone in distress.

In God's eyes, as I see Him, all errors are calls for help. And the only loving response to a call for help is forgiveness, not retaliation. It's hard for me to forgive. I never realized how hard until I tried to do it. Actually, I never realized how many bitter feelings my addiction had covered up. Now that I'm sober a few years and can reflect on my feelings toward others, I'm continually shocked at how many old grudges I still carry and how many new ones I manage to create.

Until I'm capable of more compassion, it looks like I'll need help from within, where, if I listen closely, I'll hear my Higher Power's voice. But I also have to soften my heart, not toward the whole human race necessarily, but toward each individual against whom I hold a grievance, one at a time. I know from experience that I can get help that way, for each character defect, and for each person I resent.

When I "turn you over to God," as Kathleen says, my need to judge relaxes. I experience a sudden sense of release. When I'm holding something against people, judging them by the standards of my ego, it creates a sense of strain. When I forgive them — or turn it over to God — the strain is gone and peace comes.

NOW

Prediction is a very difficult art . . . especially when it involves the future.

— *Yogi Berra*

Having spent the better part of my life trying either to relive the past or experience the future before it arrives, I have come to believe that in between those two extremes is peace. Peace comes when we live in the present.

What good does it do us to use our unique human abilities to remember and predict if it makes us unable to live in the present?

I have the nagging feeling that I've missed out on some of the best parts of my adult life. Memories of good times and bad are hard to bring into focus. Much of my early twenties, the years before I began drinking heavily, all of my thirties and part of my forties seem a shadowy world of figures in profile. I can see them darting here and there, but they won't stand still long enough for me to get a good look at them. There is a haziness about them, a sense of vagueness, and not all of it because of inebriation.

"We drink to forget," says Gertrude, a housewife and former closet drunk, "and if we drink long enough we forget without trying."

No doubt that was happening to me. Most of that part of my life was lived under the influence of alcohol. Still, my inability to recall people and events is not entirely due to foggy consciousness, blackouts, and a poor memory. Much of it is due to inattention. I was so busy looking over my shoulder, terrified that something from the past was gaining on me, or gazing fearfully into the future, expecting a catastrophe, that there was no time to devote to present living. This, combined with my alcoholic daydreams, made it impossible to experience the real world.

I don't know why I was always absent from the present. Maybe it was just anger about what had happened in the past and fear of what would happen in the future. Much of the anger and fear vanished when I sobered up and began applying to my life the Twelve Step principles of love, forgiveness, and dependence on a Higher Power. But the habit of scanning the past and the future has remained.

Live, Don't Prepare to Live

Although lacking any kind of business sense myself, I feel a kinship with people dedicated to making money. Many of them are so busy making it they don't enjoy it. They keep planning to enjoy all the luxuries their money can buy, but they never do. They are so obsessed with earning a living they forget to live. Having spent most of my life preparing to live, I understand that.

Living in the past is just as useless. To fantasize about what we wish had happened, creating happy endings for past events that went awry isn't only a waste of time, it's self-limiting and self-defeating. We are taught that those who fail to learn from history are doomed to repeat it. But often the best thing the past can teach us is that real learning takes place in the present, and understanding the present means giving it our full attention and appreciation.

From this perspective, there is no past or future since the only moment we can experience is this one. This instant is all we have. When we quit measuring ourselves by past performance we become free to enjoy what we're capable of right now.

We don't want to be judged by past mistakes. We want to be taken at face value, judged by what we have to offer at this moment. We want the benefit of a clean slate. Then why not offer the same to others and not load them down with the baggage of the past?

Marge has a reputation as a whiner and a chronic complainer. But if I don't see her as "Marge the complainer" the next time I talk to her I give myself room to see more of her. If I am having a conversation with Marge-herself-at-this-moment, instead of Marge-the-complainer, I will see a completely different person.

It takes strong will to tear our attention away from our memories of people. We have all been taught to judge people by what they have said and done in the past.

Past performance is the bread and butter of racetrack handicappers. With greyhounds, because there are no jockeys, it's everything. Handicappers have little else to go on. They become students of each dog's past. Is he a fast breaker? Can he get to the first turn quickly and avoid collisions? How well does he come from behind? Handicappers study these factors and many more.

Then a dog they picked to win loafs along and brings up the rear. The next week, this same dog, against stiffer competition, wins a race. That's why they call it gambling.

Judged on past performance, people, too, are a gamble. Each of us have good and bad days, good and bad years. Our best bet is not to judge others on their records, but assume they are loving, caring people. All we can truly know of others is what they're willing to let us see at the moment. If we can ignore our memories of them and concentrate on the here-and-now, we give people the chance to be themselves, which is exactly the same chance we want. That way we're all a sure bet.

Living in this instant, we become the personification of forgiveness. We don't have to make a conscious effort to forgive people for wrongs. They are automatically forgiven by our refusal to look at their pasts or be concerned about what they'll be like in the future. We only have to focus on this forgiving instant.

Remember what John said. "If I can't forgive, I can kiss serenity good-bye." There's no one we can't forgive if we focus on this instant. By releasing others from the past, we perceive them without blemish, as pure as they were at birth, and by doing so, we also release ourselves.

GIVE

Let no one use anything as if it were his private possession.

— *St. Ignatius of Loyola*

The first spiritual law and the one most easily tested is this: To give is to receive.

I receive what I give. As we applied it in the previous pages, forgiving others is the way our own wrongs are forgiven.

Or, what I wish for you is what I get, in one form or another.

If I'm mad at you and I feel you did something to deserve this anger, I may want you to feel terrible. But then, that's likely to be how I end up feeling too. Anger can do that. The terrible feelings I wish on you will come back to me.

Many modern psychologists put a lot of stress on releasing anger. They say that to bottle it up is to risk an emotional explosion, that it's unhealthy not to get rid of it. Feel free to express your anger, they say. But take note: while there can be a sense of relief, anger often feeds on anger.

Acknowledging and accepting the anger in ourselves is important, but only as a step to learning how to love. Psychologists have told me to express my anger. Spirituality tells me to express my love. Whatever is given is received in equal measure.

Those of us who have gained freedom from our addictions know this. We got help by helping others. We gained love by sharing love. We were released from judgment when we quit judging. We know the help, the love, and the release are not permanent; our possession of them is based on our willingness, hour by hour, to give them away.

To Give Is to Receive, To Receive Is to Give

Ask any oldtimer in our programs what to do about depression and you'll probably get the same answer: "Go help someone. You want to feel better? Try to make someone else feel better."

I am seldom overjoyed to get a phone call asking me to go on a Twelfth Step call if the person I'm supposed to see is still drinking. When an A.A. buddy and I start out on these calls, we know what we'll probably be getting into. The drunk will be feeling sorry for himself. He'll be glad that someone has taken an interest in his plight, but then he's likely to get angry. He'll tell us to mind our own business. He'll get maudlin, then angry again. And so on.

Still, I've never come away from a Twelfth Step call feeling bad. It always does something for me. I remember a man who, after begging A.A. to send someone to see him, ended up ordering us out of his house. His wife called a few months later to tell me he had drunk himself to death. I will always remember him as a man who, by receiving (although ultimately rejecting) my help, blessed me. I left his house feeling good, useful, feeling that I was fulfilling my function even though he had no idea that he was helping me.

Just as that suffering drunk wanted no part of A.A., the drunk inside me wanted no part of the idea that to keep something of value I had to give it away. That went against everything my ego stood for. My ego would tell me that to give is to suffer loss, and that the best remedy for loss is to take from someone else.

It's not a strange notion. Often in business the maxim is, "Do it to others before they can do it to you." This idea of *taking in order to have* is common in our society and explains why so many of us were often so unhappy and had no idea why. This misery stems from violating spiritual principles. To take is to lose. To do harm is to receive harm.

For many of us, ongoing recovery depends on learning that for every action there is a consequence, and that it is up to us which one we choose. With our addiction causing us to be uncommonly self-centered, it is not always easy to make the right choice.

"For me as an alcoholic," said Jeb, a twenty-five-year veteran of sobriety, "the alcohol and the way I used it was only a symptom of my underlying disease. I define that disease as self-centeredness — fear that I'm going to lose something I have or that I'm not going to get something I want."

During my first few years in recovery, I did not lightly part with the price of a fifth of bourbon or a moment of shared intimacy without wanting to know what was in it for me. It was only by watching and listening to oldtimers like Jeb that I was able to learn that giving something of value was the key to keeping it. I wanted love most of all, and little by little I saw that love came to me as I learned to give it.

"Recognize what does not matter," says *A Course in Miracles*, "and if your brothers ask you for something 'outrageous,' do it *because* it does not matter. Refuse, and your opposition establishes that it does matter to you. It is only you, therefore, who have made the request outrageous, and every request of a brother is for you. Why would you insist on denying him? For to do so is to deny yourself and impoverish both."[1]

Nothing I ever withheld brought me contentment. If I withhold love out of a desire to correct or punish, or because of indifference, I feel deprived and loveless. What I refuse to give is withheld from me.

"Everyone I Took for Granted, I Lost"

When I was first struggling to stay sober in A.A., one of the men I chose as a mentor, a man to whom I listened intently, perhaps because he took the program so seriously, was a round-faced, rosy-cheeked but dour Italian named Bill. He seldom smiled, which in my state of mind was perfectly fine. The joy of this program, for me, came later.

Bill hadn't had it easy. His was a riches to rags story, and he almost didn't make it. I could tell from the fact that, although he had been sober at least a dozen years, he was still worried about getting drunk.

---

[1] *A Course In Miracles*, vol. 1, 206. Reprinted with permission.

"Constant vigilance," Bill used to say, "is the price of sobriety." But the thing Bill said that stuck in my mind the most was this: "Everything and everyone I ever took for granted, I lost." When I take someone for granted, I am withholding both appreciation and love.

To stay sober and remain happy, I have to keep reminding myself of the first law of spirituality: To give is to receive. And its corollary: To withhold is to lose.

EVERYTHING'S OKAY

I'm okay — you're okay.

— *Thomas A. Harris*

It's okay. No matter how slow our spiritual progress may be, no matter what our opinion of how things are going, things will happen as they should.

Sure, it's frustrating to find that we often react with fear. It's discouraging that we're given to flaring up at people who can't see the logic of our arguments or who ignore our wishes. But we're beginning to see that we'll be relieved of these unwanted emotions gradually, and that we experience them for a purpose.

"Whether it's anger, frustration, anxiety, or sadness, I have to allow myself to feel those things," says Kathleen, whose recurrent theme is that she is "on time" — that she is in the place she is supposed to be and that her spiritual development is on schedule.

"The important thing is when I feel these things, not to take them out on other people. I can't. Because I'm feeling bad, I can't take it out on you. But it's okay for me to feel bad. It's okay. And what that has done for me is allow me to accept who and what I am at this moment," she adds, "and to know that I'm on time."

We need to realize that, as Kathleen says, we're doing fine where we're at right now. We don't need to worry that our spiritual growth is slow. What seems slow to us may be just right to our Higher Power.

We don't need to fret about anger and fear. As long as we know what to do about them, they cannot harm us. After acknowledging we feel anger or fear, we simply turn our attention away from them to other things, other people. We may never be rid of those emotions, but learning to deal with them can be an exercise in spiritual growth, and there is nothing more rewarding.

One thing that helps me get rid of anger is to picture my ego as one of those tiny, soprano-voiced lap dogs that go into a fit of *yap-yap-yapping*, darting around in a frenzy, *yip-yip-yip*, *yap-yap-yap*, when a stranger appears. That's what my thoughts remind me of when they smell a grievance. These thoughts race furiously from one argument to another, *yip-yip-yip*, *yap-yap-yap*, and, like mutts fighting over a fresh bone, they won't shut up until I toss them something else to gnaw on. I now know that it's possible to ignore the mutt and exercise some mental discipline, to take responsibility for my own thinking.

"Lately, I have been trying to realize and remind myself if I'm willing to treat others with forgiveness, kindness, love, and understanding, then that's the way they're going to treat me," says Ruth Ann, an alcoholic travel agent. "It's kind of selfish to look at it that way, but that's the way I want to be treated and I'm learning to treat others that way."

"It's awfully tough," she adds. "But I don't have to do these things perfectly."

If my mind is rooted in God, then I have nothing to fear from my thoughts. The only harmful thoughts come from my ego, which, after all, is my own creation. It is entirely up to me to decide what bones my mind gnaws on. My Higher Power has given me free will and won't interfere in my decisions, although His guidance is always available.

"You know," says James, the San Francisco professor, "God has given us a free will. He's given us the right to think the way we want to, but He's willing to assist us if we trust our thoughts to His care."

The idea that help with my thinking is available doesn't come readily to mind in the midst of a busy day, though. I have to keep reminding myself that it takes practice acknowledging the presence of God.

Take It From the First Person Who Flew the Atlantic

Charles Lindbergh was talking with author Jim Newton one day about their experiences with a Higher Power.

"I've found that when you make a deep commitment, unforeseen forces come to your aid," Lindbergh said. "Getting to the point of deciding is the hard part. Once you're there it's simple. I call it 'reaching the core.' [Nobel laureate scientist Alexis] Carrel calls it 'experiencing spiritual rebirth.' You call it 'listening to the inner voice.' "

"Whatever the words," Lindbergh told Newton, "I'm sure this reality is the force at the heart of the universe. That force becomes available to us in some measure, if our spirits are open to it."[1]

Jo Anne, who was a closet alcoholic, says:

"It was harder for me to say, 'I'm lonely,' than it was to say, 'I am an alcoholic.' But it was true. Since I've said that, I'm not alone anymore. And I truly feel I never have to be alone again. I have an indescribable feeling about me . . . of good . . . of a Higher Power . . . of a Source . . . that I'm not limited anymore by my own ideas. And I'm changed, too, because sometimes I'm teachable. I wanted to have all the answers. I'm grateful that I've experienced the surrender, humility, and the peace that comes from not having to have all the answers."

For addicts making a commitment to the spiritual life, the rewards come and lives change in unexpected ways. We grow gradually. Seldom is it a smooth, upward climb. It may be two steps forward and one backward, or one forward and two backward. But most of us slowly learn to distinguish the voice of our Higher Power from the voice of our ego.

My life has become satisfying. I feel longer periods of calm and shorter periods of anger and fear. I believe that I'm on schedule with my spiritual growth and will always be if I depend on the guidance of my Higher Power. I have learned to accept that there is a purpose in the gradual unfolding rather than a sudden revelation of His will for me. A sudden, miraculous revelation of His will is no longer necessary.

Even if my wish for permanent peace and serenity were suddenly granted, I wouldn't know what to do with it. I'm here to

---

[1] Newton, Jim, *Uncommon Friends* (New York: Harcourt, Brace, & Jovanovich, 1987), 163.

work through the problems of the individual I am, negative feelings and all. And as I accept help in working them out, I may do something to help someone else.

My reason for being on earth may be obscure, but my function is not. My function is to be myself, to be loving, to forgive. If I can learn that and impart it to someone else, my mission will be accomplished. Then, whatever happens, it's okay. How can it be otherwise?

SUMMARY

THE PROBLEM
(What Ails Us)

1. Self-centered in the extreme, most of us are convinced we'll be all right if we can just get more — more of anything to make us look better and feel better. Our disease is the idea that salvation lies in getting "more."
2. Those of us who have devoted our lives to indulging our senses have come to realize that the pleasures of the material world are temporary and that they hold nothing of lasting value. They have left us hungering for something of substance, which we can find, in the spiritual world.

THE ANALYSIS
(Some Things That Look Promising)

1. This strange, new, spiritual world, however, does not automatically transform us. We discover that our character defects are still with us, and that if we are to lose our anger and fear, it takes more than simple faith.
2. We have seen that love works miracles, but that coming to terms with it is not a simple matter.
3. Where do we turn for spiritual instruction? All of us are teachers as well as students. We find that we learn from each other as we teach each other.
4. We also learn that people appear when we need them, and that spiritual progress is inevitable if we trust them — while practicing the Twelve Steps.

THE SOLUTION
(Ways to Give Progress a Nudge)

1. Putting them into action is the way to discover if our principles for living are worth anything. Before they can work for us, the Twelve Steps must be applied to our daily activities.
2. "Acting as if" is a perfect substitute for faith. It is, in fact, the best way to find out if skepticism is justified. The results are surprising.
3. Making a decision to let our Higher Power handle our affairs, hour by hour, and more often as needed, is an act that has the power to transform our lives.
4. Showing appreciation is appropriate for every person we encounter. It is the logical substitute for judgment, which will always be faulty.
5. Asking for help releases us from self-centeredness and restores the bonds to our sisters and brothers.
6. Whatever our problems, we have to work them out in the company of people, for answers come not in isolation, but from and through our brothers and sisters.
7. Taking down our defenses is the most protective thing we can do.
8. Forgiveness is a healing act. It is the appropriate response to all acts of hostility, which are only calls for help.
9. This instant is the only time we have. Living in it — instead of the past and future — brings us freedom.
10. To give is to receive.
11. Everything is okay. It helps us to see that in the spiritual world, we're where we're supposed to be and on time.

THE TWELVE STEPS°

1. We admitted we were powerless over (fill in your addiction) — that our lives had become unmanageable.
2. Came to believe that a Power greater than ourselves could restore us to sanity.
3. Made a decision to turn our will and our lives over to the care of God *as we understood Him.*
4. Made a searching and fearless moral inventory of ourselves.
5. Admitted to God, to ourselves, and to another human being the exact nature of our wrongs.
6. Were entirely ready to have God remove all these defects of character.
7. Humbly asked Him to remove our shortcomings.
8. Made a list of all persons we had harmed, and became willing to make amends to them all.
9. Made direct amends to such people whenever possible, except when to do so would injure them or others.
10. Continued to take personal inventory and when we were wrong promptly admitted it.
11. Sought through prayer and meditation to improve our conscious contact with God *as we understood Him,* praying only for knowledge of His will for us and the power to carry that out.
12. Having had a spiritual awakening as the result of these steps, we tried to carry this message to (addicts), and to practice these principles in all our affairs.

THE TWELVE STEPS OF
ALCOHOLICS ANONYMOUS*

1. We admitted we were powerless over alcohol — that our lives had become unmanageable.
2. Came to believe that a Power greater than ourselves could restore us to sanity.
3. Made a decision to turn our will and our lives over to the care of God *as we understood Him.*
4. Made a searching and fearless moral inventory of ourselves.
5. Admitted to God, to ourselves, and to another human being the exact nature of our wrongs.
6. Were entirely ready to have God remove all these defects of character.
7. Humbly asked Him to remove our shortcomings.
8. Made a list of all persons we had harmed, and became willing to make amends to them all.
9. Made direct amends to such people wherever possible, except when to do so would injure them or others.
10. Continued to take personal inventory and when we were wrong promptly admitted it.
11. Sought through prayer and meditation to improve our conscious contact with God *as we understood Him,* praying only for knowledge of His will for us and the power to carry that out.
12. Having had a spiritual awakening as the result of these steps, we tried to carry this message to alcoholics, and to practice these principles in all our affairs.

---

*The Twelve Steps are taken from *Alcoholics Anonymous* (Third Edition), published by A.A. World Services, Inc., New York, N.Y., pp. 59-60. Reprinted with permission.

Index

A.A. *See* Alcohlics Anonymous

A Course in Miracles, 29, 39-40, 51-52, 62, 68

Acting as if, 17-22

Action-taking, 23-26

Addictive personality, 2

Alcoholics Anonymous, 13

Alcoholics Anonymous: learning cycle in, 31-32; love and brotherhood in, 37-38

Altruism, 38-40

Anger, 35

Appreciation, of people, 51-53

Belief, lack of, 21-22

Belonging, feeling of, 51

Bill W., 21-28; *Twelve Steps and Twelve Traditions,* 34

Brotherhood, in Alcoholics Anonymous, 37

Change: achievement of, through Twelve Steps, 17; recognizing need for, 2

Conflicts, spiritual guidance during, 67-68

Craziness. *See* Insanity

Defenselessness, 67-70

Defenses, dropping of, 69-70

Detinger, Friedrich, 1

Ego. *See* Mighty Ego

Ego trap, 53

Eleventh Step, The, 2-3, 11, 14, 35

Faith, lack of, 21-22

Fear, 35

Fifth Step, The, 12

Forgiveness, 71-74

Friendship, 5

Fosdick, Emerson, 29

Fox, Emmet, 29

Giving, 55, 79-82

Gray, Glenn J.: The Warriors: Reflections on Men in Battle, 39

Higher Power: and the Mighty Ego, 45; communication with, 2

Holmes, Ernest, 29

Humility, 46, 73

Insanity, admission of, 17-19

Jampolsky, Gerald G.: *Love is Letting Go of Fear,* 31, 35

Jung, Carl, 71

Language, and spirituality, 57-59

Late Night Thoughts on Listening to Mahler's Ninth Symphony, 38

Learning: cycle, 30-32; process in recovery, 23

Living, in the present, 75-77

Love: and fear, 36; giving in to, 39-41; in Alcoholics Anonymous, 37-38; resolving conflicts through, 69-70

Love is Letting Go of Fear, 31, 35

Mighty Ego, 43-45

Nature, Man and Woman, 68

Need, for others, 61-62

Negative emotions, dealing with, 83-86

Niebuhr, Reinhold, 1

Nonjudgemental attitude, 51

Other-direction, 61-62

Peale, Norman Vincent, 29

Recovery: and Twelve Steps, 2-3;
    intellectual approach to, 20-21;
    changes in recovering addicts, 13
Responsiblity, for own actions, 64

Second Step, The, 14, 17-18
Self-acceptance, 71-73
Serenity Prayer, The, 1
Sixth Step, The, 33
Sobriety, achievement of, 3
Spiritual growth, 8; and the
    Eleventh Step, 2-3
Spiritual guidance, during conflicts,
    67-68
Spiritual literature, 28-29
Spiritual world, 8

The Grapevine, 28
The Eleventh Step, 2-3, 11, 14, 35
The Fifth Step, 12
The Second Step, 14, 17-18
The Serenity Prayer, 1
The Sixth Step, 33
The Third Step, 14, 45
The Twelfth Step, 14
*The Warriors: Reflections on Men
    in Battle*, 39
Thomas, Lewis: *A Course in
    Miracles*, 39-40; *Late Night
    Thoughts on Listening To
    Mahler's Ninth Symphony*, 38
Trust, 65
Twelfth Step, The, 14
Twelve Step programs, 8-9, 12, 31
Twelve Steps, 3, 13, 17-18, 31
*Twelve Steps and Twelve Tradi-
    tions*, 34

Watts, Alan W.: *Nature, Man and
    Woman*, 68

Other titles that will interest you...

The Twelve Steps
A Healing Journey

The revealing, moving narrative of a recovering alcoholic who dared to go deep within himself, wrestle with his human failings, and discover his own spiritual voice. *The Twelve Steps: A Healing Journey* can help you look within yourself and find the presence of your Higher Power. You'll not only read about conscious contact with God, you'll begin to sense unconscious contact with God. 63 pp.

Order No. 5175

Conscious Contact
Partnership with a Higher Power
by Gail N.

A practical, inspiring look at spiritual experience, this pamphlet describes alternative perceptions of a Higher Power and ways to improve our conscious contact with God, as we understand God. 24 pp.

Order No. 5250

Women and Spirituality
by Jeanne E.

As recovering women, our relationship with a Higher Power requires particular work and attention. The author combines guidelines and ideas for shaping a meaningful, fulfilling image of a Higher Power with the experiences of other recovering women to help us find the special, spiritual Power that fits our own individual rhythms of life. 20 pp.

Order No. 5561

For price and order information please call one of our Customer Service Representatives
HAZELDEN EDUCATIONAL MATERIALS
(800) 328-9000   **(800) 257-0070**   **(612) 257-4010**
(Toll Free, U.S. Only)   (Toll Free, MN Only)   (AK and outside U.S.)
Pleasant Valley Road, Box 176, Center City, MN 55012-0176